TITLE: Raised By Wolves, the Shawn Khalifa story.

TITLE:

ROBERT JONES GONE FISHING (Book One)

DEDICATION: To my most wonderful daughter Jennifer Ponce and son Shawn Khalifa without them my life would not be complete. Like all mothers my children are my life. Also this dedication includes my grandson Jackson Ponce who makes the world go round.

PROLOGUE

Death is the ultimate in rudeness. I loved you and you left me; I laughed with you and you left me: I was your friend, your partner in crime and you left me; part of my smile was yours and yours was mine. We resembled each other, we laughed a like, we laughed a lot, and we thought alike, we truly liked each other. Our admiration for each other was mutual. What was perceived as appalling to others, was the catalyst for our humor. I can truly say, my Brother Bob's humor is what brought me happiness all through my childhood. Death is an everlasting rudeness, a rudeness for which no apology exits.

When I looked at his swollen stomach, his unseeing eyes and his face that didn't resemble my brother listening to his last struggling breaths, I felt anger. How he dare leave me, we promised always to take care of each other. The promise was never in words it was in being. He was my brother, my baby, my protector and my friend and I felt like he was going home before the game was over. The feeling of anger was surreal because I couldn't ever get even with him for leaving far too early.

I remember when my dad was dying of cancer. I would sit by his bedside and we would pass the time, like two people waiting for a table in a too crowded restaurant. We watched the news, he no longer cared about the stock market or too much of the future. He once said to me, "Colleen it's hard to die". In all the months I visited him he only said it once and that was all that was needed to communicate what he wanted me to know. It was the only time he alluded to the fact he was dying. It was a part of life that we both acknowledged and accepted. I remember feeling bad because his handsomeness was gone. He was still here, he was still my father and he was gone. I truly believed my father was a saint. He accepted his pain as part of his lot, and bare it as he envisioned Jesus endured his pain on the cross.

I believe even the most devout are stricken with periods of panic, which are laden with agnosticism. What I am about to write about are my experiences. If I were to read this re-counting,

I too would be very skeptical. So I don't blame you if you think I am a nut, because I would feel the same way myself. That's why it has been twelve years and even though I am compelled, possibly driven to re-count these episodes I am also reluctant. Please have patience, because I am not a writer as my son Shawn Khalifa is, or would I pretend to have such a Novel ability.

The children in my family were born and raised Catholic, the nun's taught us that it was impossible for the dead to communicate with the living. Our faith and blind belief would eventually bring us home to Jesus. We believed it was most unusual but occasionally communication, from the dead to the living occurred.

I do remember somewhere between the horror stories of nun's being beaten with hoses, after the hoses were forced down their throats and their bodies filled with water and the evil spirits taking a baby to the cellar and setting fire to the bed, it was laid upon, that we were taught that spirits were known to communicate with loved ones left behind. This of course was very rare and only happened on some saintly level. My insight was it could never happen to a soul as lowly as mine with the little black and gray marks polka dots all over it, from many sins. Oh! The mental damage that can be brought about in the guise of religion.

I remember the first time a nun was talking about death and I guess I became aware of my own mortality, I saw black. I remember returning home from school and asking my mom, "Why are we here if we are just going to die someday".

Her answer was, to have babies". I think I was about 10 years old, I thought, "Why would anyone bring babies into this world to love, knowing they were destined to die". For literally years after this incident, I went into a deep depression. It began with hiding in cupboards or sitting in corners. I imagined a gray mass in my stomach, hind sight now suggests that this was probably feelings of dismay and anxiety over the realization of my own mortality. I kept imaging a gray mass in my gut, wishing it could be washed clean or cut out of my stomach. It got so bad that when anyone in my family was away from the house. I would estimate the time for them to arrive home and watch the clock. I would start to watch out of a window that was positioned to see the entrance of our street and with every passing minute of their expected time of arrival, I would pray with each passing headlight that it was them, always imagining the worst, vacillating between hope and fear. If a half an hour passed, I would start walking up and down the streets crying, dodging the oncoming headlights, hiding behind whatever was available, praying it was them and at the same time not wanting to be found in my crazed state. These paranoia's stayed with me to various degrees for years. I was petrified and preoccupied with death. If I passed a mortuary or God forbid a hearse would pass me by I would go into a deep depression and the gray feeling would start to manifest in my stomach and the imaginary mass would grow.

My dad had a major heart attach when he was 38 years old. His stay in the veterans' hospital lasted over a year. The time frame was around the time by-pass surgery was being pioneered and the mortality rate wasn't desirable. His option was to become semi invalid. He was watching a special on TV which was asking for individuals in his position to volunteer to take an experimental drug. At that time he was told that he had less than a year to live, so he decided nobly to become a human Guinea pig for persons possible his children or grandchildren that find themselves in his same predicament. Anyway the drug was a bust and the mortality rate was very high, in patients that death wasn't execrated, strokes became predominate. My father suffered a stroke that lasted for three hours. When he recounted his experiences to me they went something like this.

"I remember waking up and faces were all around me, they were talking and I started to understand what they were saying.

"Call the priest he's going". I thought to myself I am not going anywhere, there is nothing wrong with me. I tried to talk to them and let them know they were wrong. I was all right. I heard an animal noise, a weird animal noise, it sounded like gurgling and moaning at the same time. I suddenly realized that noise was coming from me. I tried to move my hands, my feet, lift my head and nothing moved. I began to feel trapped like the animal I sounded like, powerless and exhausted from the fight. Later some nurses were working over my bed and I heard them say,

"Well, I guess they will move him to a convalescent home, he's a vegetable now". I swear, my mind was never sharper all I could envision was that I would lay in my own internal hell for the rest of my life. The anger I felt was beyond any emotion I have ever experienced. I would lay existing being treated and taken care of as a nonexistent, a chore an inanimate object. By the way, 3 years later he had by-pass surgery and lived a very active and normal life for another 28 years.

When my brother discovered he was terminal he called me and said,

"Colleen I want to come home to die".

Home of course was with me. He had a saying, "I want to die with a beer in my hand and my feet in the sand", and we would laugh. He almost made it. Of course, you don't just go sit in a beach chair, close your eyes and your dead. No, there is no choice or dignity in dying. The second to last time I saw my brother alive, his cataract covered eyes were staring without emotion, he didn't respond. I went home feeling as if he were already gone, it was just a matter of time before this would become a reality. His greatest fear was dying alone, I wanted to let him know I was with him. I don't mean I wanted to die with him. I wanted to somehow let him know I was with him when he made his transition.

In the middle of the night. I woke up from a sound sleep remembering my dad's experience and how his mind worked while his body didn't. I would buy my brother a tape player and ear phones. The next day I couldn't wait until the stores opened. I bought his favorite music, Bob loved music. Janis Joplin was one of his favorites. I took the tapes to him and put the ear phones on him and blared the music. I still could not see any awareness in his eyes but in his lips I saw recognition. When I removed his ear phones too change tapes. I could detect a slight quiver in the edges of his lips and they would form a slight pout. This was the pout that got him everything he wanted when we were kids.

The evening after my brother passed I was holding a pack of cigarettes in my hand standing by the microwave in the kitchen staring at the wall. The cigarette Package started to move.

I asked, "If you are my brother go to the microwave, if you are not go to the salt shaker".

The package went to the microwave. I know this is certifiable and as the years pass I question the validity myself but at the time I ran to get my mom.

"Bob is in the cigarette package", I said.

I made a make shift wee gee board with a crystal glass and torn up pieces of paper. The glass whizzed around the letters spelling out words.

"YOU ARE MY SISTER AND I LOVE YOU, STOP SMOKING".

CHAPTER ONE

Eileen and I were born August 17, 1947. Bob was born Sept. 21 1948, I guess this is known as Irish triplets. Even though Bob was only 13 months younger than us, he was our baby for as long as I can remember, my first vivid memory of him was when I was about 3 years old. We were in the car waiting for our mom who was at the Marine Base medical center at a doctor's appointment. I guess in those days it was socially acceptable to leave small children alone in cars, because I remember being left alone in the car a lot. Anyway, Bobby is standing up at the window with his little hands curled around the top looking out, when a woman comes up to the car she has a service uniform on.

She says, "What a cute little boy".

Bobby looks up at her with his cute little dimples and beautiful twinkling blue eyes and says,

"Get out of here you poo poo marine woman".

The look on the woman's face as she stood there huffing, gave me my first real belly laugh. This set the venue for the rest of our lives. Bob looked like an angel, people were drawn to him like a magnet. He was clever and thought up the most outrageous pranks and in most cases got away with just short of murder. Me on the other hand looked just like the devil I was and always got caught.

I remember when I was in the fourth grade and Bob was in the third he came into my classroom during recess and got me.

"You want to see my arsenal", he asked.

He took me into his class room and showed me three rows of buggers under his desk.

"See that stupid ugly girl by the trash can, she keeps smiling and talking to me she thinks I like her. When she's not looking I flick my buggers at her".

Sure enough you could see dried buggers around her desk. This row is the greenies, they are the ones I picked today, the second row is almost ready and the last one is just right for shooting.

He demonstrated by flicking a dried one, which landed on her seat. He knew I loved a good bugger joke. In those days there was nothing funnier to me than buggers. I laughed every time I saw that girl thinking of those big old dried buggers.

Bob grew to be a womanizer, oh how he loved his women. On his first day of kindergarten we went home on the bus and it smelled like shit. When we got off the bus Bobby ran home leaving behind a smelly trail. Later, he told me that when my mom look him to school and left him off he was crying. He was mad because there was snot all over his face and the other kids saw him crying. The desks were the old fashioned wooden ones where the seats lift up. He saw the other kids sitting down, he kept pulling and pulling on the seat and it wouldn't come down. He pulled so hard he pooped his pants, this made him cry even harder. The cute little girl behind him, simply walked up and lowered the seat for him. She sat holding hands with him all the home stinky pants and all. Throughout his life Bob was in love, his love escapades were famous to all who knew him.

I could go on with Bob stories forever but will not subject you to too many more. I would like to tell you a few more, hopefully just enough to set the mood for the rest of the story and have you in-tune to where we were coming from. Our family is typical with characters similar to all of yours and experiences that may mirror some of your own.

I can never say I was the best kid in the world but I had a lot of fun and laughter as I grew into who I became as an adult. Again a story, I remember this teacher's pet who sat behind me in 2nd grade. She kept tapping me on the shoulder. I turned around and she showed me her new pig eraser.

I asked her, "Can I see your pig eraser"? She handed it to me which really surprised me, most kids would have said no. They probably would have figured I would have bit the head off or something. Later that day I noticed I still had the pig eraser on my desk. I turned around to the girl figuring she would know I was kidding, I said,

"Hey, look I've got a pig eraser just like yours".

"Really" she said, "I lost mine".

"Oh, that's too bad", I said.

"I will sell you my pig eraser for a nickel".

Her smile became really big and she handed me the nickel. That was the day I realized that there were some good unsuspecting people on this earth and then there are people like me.

My next big lesson came again in Catholic grade school. I think I was in the fourth grade. My friend wanted to swing and all the swings were taken, she stood behind a cubby little girl and started to count her out. Once she reached a certain number the other girl was supposed to give up her turn. The girls name was Carolyn, she got straight A's and was an obvious favorite of the teachers.

"Well" good little Carolyn said, "You can't make me get off the fucking swing" You could hear all of the kids gasp, as their faces turned bright red. What is this new word that got such a reaction, I wondered?

"FUCK", I said, really loud taking the attention off of Carolyn.

"You shouldn't say that Colleen", one of the kids yelled.

"You're going to hell".

Carolyn threw up her middle finger and waved it in my face. All of the kids reacted, wow this was right up my alley; anytime I could punch the ball away when another kid who was trying to catch it or jump into a game of jump rope and ruin the count, I got tickled. I loved teasing the other kids and messing with their games. I entertained myself by pinching my twin sister or wiping buggers on her making her scream, after all we did not have video games in those days and my parents were too poor to buy us toy's. The more my sister screamed the more my nose would wrinkle up and I'd get tickled. I guess you could say I was the bad twin. Whenever my nose started to wrinkle the other kids became conditioned to run for cover. So when Carolyn threw that middle finger up, my nose definitely started to wrinkle up and I threw my middle finger up right back at her. When recess ended I tapped the girl in front of me and wrote, "fuck" at the top of my paper.

I whispered to her, "What does that mean"? SHIT, she wrote back. This was even better than I could imagine. I started pointing my middle finger at the floor.

I told my partner in crime, "If you make the shit sign to the devil you will never go to hell".

We sat the rest of the afternoon making the shit sign to the floor until the bell rang. Our teacher, a big fat nun wiggled her way down the aisle to Janiece and my seats,

"You two stay after school", she bellowed.

Janiece had to stay outside while I talked to her first.

"Greg Able told me that you were making obscene jesters and saying vulgar words". I didn't know what obscene meant or vulgar, but I could easily figure out it was my new found work FUCK AND MY NEW FRIEND THE MIDDLE FINGER that she was talking about. Greg was the nastiest kid in the class. What I remember most about him is he looked like a chicken and always looked up girl's dresses.

I felt his betrayal was despicable and unforgiveable. The word fuck was right up his alley, another lesson, I would have never believed Greg to be petty and low enough to instigate our demise. I also, will always believe the word fuck did not offend him or he did not squeal to save our souls, as the nun suggested strongly. I could have been walking the plank, with the feeling of dread I felt as I approached the stone goddess of nunnery.

"Greg has reported you for using a horrible rude word. He is ashamed and disgusted that you know or used that word; your poor sister would be so embarrassed if she knew. Now tell me the word you were using", I could not for the life of me say "FUCK" to a nun,

"I will write it, I won't say it".

She handed me a pen and paper and I wrote FUCK across the paper.

"What does it mean", she said sternly. In my agitated state her big face looming with vaguely distorted features like looking through the fish eye len of a camera.

"It means "Shit", I say.

"Who taught you that word"?

"I heard Carolyn use it on the playground".

"You're lying, Carolyn is a good girl, and she would never use that word. How dare you try to get her into trouble".

"Okay, I say it was Janiece who taught me the word".

"That's more like it she replied, not only are you rude and use dirty words, you are a liar on top of it. For the life of me I don't know what to do with you. I will not shame our parents by telling them what despicable acts you have done, their disappointment would be too great, but I warn you if I ever hear of a hint of such indiscretion again your parents will be called immediately". Boy what a relief, I was given a reprieve, the immediate feeling of exhilaration was gratifying. I felt I had gotten away with something monumental. Another lesson, perception is reality. One would think that such life lessons at such an early age would prepare me for the events in this Book, but sadly it didn't.

When I got home, I found Bobby the all-knowing.

"Fuck, does not mean shit", he told me in his infinite wisdom.

"Fuck means when a man and a woman put their pee together and a baby comes out".

I don't remember who talked who into it, but we went into the bathroom to make a baby. One of us peed first and the other followed. We watching intently, expecting a baby to form. After a while we got bored and went off to play, checking periodically to see if a baby had come. I remember, my sister Eileen wanted to use the bathroom (in those days there was only one in most houses), and we would not let her, we told her to go outside and pee in the yard because we didn't want her to be part of our baby. She went crying to our mom. Mom immediately went into the bathroom and flushed the toilet.

The dynamics of our childhood patterned the old classic movie, Trouble with Angels. We were both Mary Clancy's suffering flagrant injustices, because of our scaling brilliant ideas.

CHAPTER TWO

Bob left our family home as I did at age 17. We were both independent and strong willed people. Bob married a beautiful girl named Kathi Friedman, much to the horror of her parents. He lived in her closet with their pet raccoon for six months prior to their wedding. Bob and Cathy had a beautiful little daughter. They were picture perfect, blond, and blue eyed and beautiful. They left California for Oregon, without a destination or a clue as to what the future would bring. They had smiles, they had love, they had adventure and they had grit. Bob's deep love and devotion for his daughter Anne was insurmountable, she was his all. The happiness she brought him was over whelming. Even in moments of deep despair, just the mention of Ann's name would bring a smile too his lips. There was a glow of happiness that radiated from him whenever he spoke of her, she was definitely his pride and joy. After Bob and Kathi moved away it would be another twenty years before we were to be together again.

In my early twenties I began to experience my first paranormal episodes. Pretty common really, reoccurring dreams that cast a glimpse into the future. The dream was always a distorted version of reality. Sometimes I would feel sharp pains in my right knee, only later to learn that my twin sister had arthritis in the same knee and was in a great deal of pain. We also were separated for many years. It is amazing how our lives have paralleled aside from feeling each other's physical pain. I remember one peculiar incidence, I believe it changed my life. I was about 20 years old, sharing an apartment with a good high school friend. I remember lying on the couch and watching a game show; Burt Reynolds was the guest. The next thing I knew I was floating above my body. I vaguely remember an over whelming feeling of relief because I was still myself, I could see my body lying on the couch. I remember my legs were crossed and I thought I don't need those legs, I don't even need the body I cared so much about. I didn't feel sad because I didn't have my body anymore. I felt whole. I existed but I was not physical, an entity maybe with no form. I was really excited. I saw my friend, I wanted to tell her. I could not get her attention, I felt like I was screaming but she was totally unaware of my presence or the being I had become. Floating close to her head, I immediately got scared, was I going to float around in my own apartment not to be heard? For how long? Could this last forever? I panicked and started to fight. There was no dead relatives to greet me, there was no glowing light to go to, just an incredible feeling of aloneness. I remember thinking, "I am not positive enough to die, let me be more positive, let me be more ready to die". There is no way of describing the incredible strength it took to get back into my body. The only way to explain it is to say I literally willed myself back. I was devastated and weak for weeks after the experience. My sister Eileen at the time was practicing astral projection and her explanation for my out of body experience was that she triggered it.

There is a man and on rare occasions he contacts me in my dreams. I recognize know and accept him. My best guess is he has contacted me four times in my life. It's weird but I have never been shown the really good things that have happened to me, only the devastating things, things that I mentally don't know how I would have gotten through them without him. The first

time I saw him was when I was nineteen years old.
There was a girl in my school her name was Dee
Dee Daily. She was younger than I am by a year. I
remember seeing her at school she was a cute girl,
always laughing with her friends. I should look
her up on face book to see if she is still alive. I did
not know her she was not even an acquaintance
of mine. After I graduated from high school, I saw
her in line at the bank. A feeling of anguish and
dread washed over me, her presence made me
feel physically sick. Several weeks later a friend
was talking to me and she said,

"You know Dee Dee Daily, it's really sad, she
has multiple sclerosis". Horror engulfed me. I
was perplexed, I didn't even know this girl. I
should have felt sad as I would about anyone who
fell on hard times, but the feelings I was having
were total out of proportion. I almost felt like her
disease was a part of me. I started having
nightmares and would see her face in my dreams.
I would feel sick and depressed for days after each
dream. The dreams became a reality. I started
seeing Dee Dee around town. Each time I would
see her the feeling of being emotionally and

physically sick became worse, just as her disease appeared to be becoming worse.

I saw her again at the bank, her eyes appeared unfocused and she was using a cane. I went to see a house that I was interested in renting, and who was coming out of the house, Dee Dee, it was almost as if she were haunting me. I became obsessed with her, dreading trips to the bank; dreading going to sleep at night. It all ended just a just as fast as it began. I had a dream one night, I saw the man, he said simply, "Don't worry Dee Dee is okay and I became okay again. ·

The same friend that told me of Dee Dee visited again, this time she said,

"You know Dee Dee Daily". I already knew what she was going to say, "She is okay the doctors say it's a miracle she has nothing wrong with her, her disease just went away".

The next time I saw the man I was about five years older. I had an intense dream. My friend was flying an airplane, my mom was sitting in the back seat. I remember the plane starting going down and we were spinning in circles about to reach the ground when the earth that we were heading towards changed and the man's face appeared before me,

"It's not your time he said", and I guess I woke up. Years later my husband and I were taking a trip at Christmas in a single engine Cessna, in the back seat was my one year old daughter. I was dozing when I was rudely awakened by my husband's scream.

"We are in a flying coffin", he yelled into the mike. I looked at the instruments and they were moving in circles. I should have been terrified, I wasn't. I instinctively know it was not my time. We had hit icing conditions and had fallen below the terrain, it took three airliners, a helicopter and many air traffic controllers to bring us in. We made it, it was not my time, just as he had said, if I had not previously experienced the premonition, I would have died of fright for my little family.

The next experience I had was not the man. The face of the man is nice; it is kind. This person was a pie face, perfectly round. My dad was dying of cancer and the pie man came to me one night. I felt dread when I saw him, he wanted me to fly with him. I didn't want to go. It still makes me sad when I remember. I knew he wanted to tell me my dad would be leaving us. He flew me to a place that was covered by slats, like a wall. They reminded me of huge venetian blinds. We said nothing, there was only silence but somehow he was communicating with me and I understood perfectly what his message was, there was something almost forbidden in what he was to show me. Somehow I understood all I could see was a glimpse. He moved one of the blinds aside and I saw the most incredible light. It made me feel good, I wanted more, but I knew I couldn't have it, I was only supposed to observe, I was not part of what I was seeing. The light was happiness, it was love.

CHAPTER THREE

Life was good to me, I felt so blessed, I had two beautiful children and a lot of love. I was forty three and staying at my mom's house overnight when the phone call came, my brother Bob was gravely ill. My mom flew up to be with him. He started hemorrhaging and it was thought at first that he had ulcers. It turned out to be a very nasty disease called aplastic anemia. Children are sometimes born with the disease. Bob got it from a horse medication called Butte. He was a horse trainer, famous in his own right. For two years we lived on pins and needles waiting for his phone calls to report the progress of his disease. It was like a roller coaster. Sometimes he was making platelets and we would be encouraged, then the next report would come and he was dangerously low and needed a transfusion. Those familiar with the disease know that its victims literally stay alive with transfusions.

Bob called me several years into his disease and said,

"The doctors say its time, I am going to die and I want to come home". And of course home was with me. The Lord was kind we had Bob with us for another six years.

When we were children, Bob fought my battles. I would antagonize and exasperate others just to the point of explosion and then run for cover. I felt braver when Bob was around because I could push the envelope just a little bit further and if the results ended in any real trouble, I would run to Bob with whatever story I could conger up and he be would beat up my alleged assailant. After Bob came to live with me as weak, blind, and crippled as he got he still continued to fight my battles.

For years I had a reoccurring dream about a snake in a pool. My family would be staying at a hotel. It was summer time. I would walk through some trees and come upon a pool. The water in the pool was black and forbidding; in the pool is a big black ugly snake. How Freudian is that? I am petrified of the snake and a feeling of hate washes over me. I reluctantly peer closer into the pool and something about the ugly snake fascinates me. There is just a hint of kindness that I see in the snake. My fear turns to curiosity as I openly confront the evil entity, mesmerized I am drawn to the creature under its hideous exterior, is good. He, makes me feel comfortable, he is my friend. I feel safe in his presence, I am protected and I am loved.

I had these dreams until the time I met and fell in love with my husband. I always believed and still do that he was my snake. I fell in love with him at first sight. My mother, my siblings and my friends did not like him. He entertained me and was extremely intelligent, yet he could be the most naïve person, almost to the point of being mentally handicapped I have ever known. In all reality he was evil un-personified, and yet he was remarkably kind. He was a great airline pilot, could speak 5 languages and played every instrument he touched. He was amazing and extremely complex, yet I felt comfortable and secure in his presence at the same time he was a threat to my basic existence. His father was Gilly Gilly a famous magician, if you are old enough you may remember his performance on the Ed Sullivan show in the late 60's.

Hamdi's background was theatrical, his Aunt was a famous movie star in Egypt, and her name was Niama Akef. I married Hamdi, not even knowing who he was. As sad as it is, I fell in love with and married an illusion. I believed he was father knows best, the dad in Leave It To Beaver. I perceived as true the fallacy he had created for himself, innocence is not always your best friend.

CHAPTER-4

It was a quiet warm evening and as was our custom Bob and I were sitting next to the fireplace, starting into the first beers of the evening. It was about 75 degrees outside but Bob was now always cold. As I gazed at his still handsome face thoughts of his latest womanizing crept into my head. Several months before I started up the stairs to put cloths away in the bedroom, I had to walk around Bob who was sitting on the large landing just before the steps turn to go upstairs. His blue eyes were twinkling and his dimples were deep. I looked beyond his gaze and saw a beautiful Mexican girl seated on the top stairs, skirt hiked up with her, let's say her honey pot, love muffin, whatever you want to call it exposed in all its glory. My children play on these stairs, it took me three hours the next day to scrub them down.

One very hot summer day, we were at the lake, Bob kept nudging me from the side.

"Get away from me", he whispered. What I saw, when I looked up was several dazzling beauties glancing his way.

"If they think we're married they'll never come over, go away". I dug my heels in and yelled to one of the ten kids we had with us.

"Come over and let daddy put lotion on you" He was pissed, I could see his brow furrow as his discontentment increased. He finally gave into the fact that I wasn't going to move my big fat white butt anywhere and eventually his good humor returned. All of a sudden his dimples deepened and his smile widened, I turned just in time to see a women clad in a skimpy bikini approaching us.

"Can you do me a favor", she purred to my brother,

"Would you", she said as she pivoted around with all the grace of a French runway model,

"Check out my ass and see if it's too old for this suit". What suit? Her ass was completely hanging out, I swear the hairs around her anus were peeking out of the only covering the suit provided. I saw this as she sort of rotated around thrusting her protruding backside several inches from Bob face.

"My family is jealous", she slurred indication she may have had a wee bit too much to drink,

"They say my butt has dents in it. Does it have dents huh"?

"Your butt is perfectly fine, it looks great, yes a great ass to me", Bob retorted, definitely in his element. She did a little bow, further thrusting her precious treasures closer to Bob's face, she straightened and sauntered off ass swaying in the breeze. We looked at each other and simultaneously let go of the laughter that was building up in our bellies.

Another incident that always tickles me happened during one the most troublesome experiences of my life. We were at the family law center getting an emergency restraining order against my husband. At first I was very stressed, I had never done anything like this in my life and didn't know what to expect or what I was doing. I kept standing in lines and every time it was my turn I was doing something wrong and had to start over. To say the least, it was not a good day and I was not in a good mood. In my tenth line when I glanced at the women next to me, she was rather cute, and had on revealing cut offs, her body was the kind that I wished I had hidden under my cloths. She seemed unaware of her perfectly tanned legs as her piercing blue troubled eyes glanced around the room. I swear like magnets they connected with my brothers. He gave her his equally cute, softly understanding smile welcoming her silently to share her troubles with him. She looked mesmerized as she approached him. She sat down next to him, they looked like they belonged together, two of the beautiful people. From my vantage point I could see they were smiling and looking into each other's eyes. How nauseating had he no shame, this was the worst day of my life and he was totally enjoying himself. Bob could comfort a beautiful woman, the way a Hershey's with almonds comforts me. All of a sudden my mood started to elevate, I liked nothing better than to tease Bob. A sadistic plan began to form in my head.

"Kids", I called to my two children. "I will take you to McDonalds if you run over to Uncle Bob and say Daddy, can we go to McDonalds"?

The kids needed no persuasion; my kids will sell their souls for McDonalds. They ran over, jumped on Bob and did the dirty deed. By the end of the charade Bob was scowling and my kids were clinging to him, I was tickled to the foundation of my soul and cutie pie was walking away. Bob looked over calculating the level of my, got ya and could only laugh.

Sorry I got off on a tangent. If you remember Bob and I were sitting in front of the fire in the beginning of this chapter, I was sort of day dreaming I think what triggered it was appreciating the fact that Bob was still a nice looking man, despite the increasing frailties he was experiencing from the eminent progression of his disease. Desperado was playing in the background. He looked solemn as the fire brightened his cheeks.

"Colleen its time, I need to come down from my fence and let somebody love me, before it's too late". A feeling of doom washed over me, as I thought to myself, it's already too late. The contrast of his Marlboro man appearance and the awareness that he was deteriorating insides made the realization even harder to bear.

"You know we should have been the twins, you're the only one that understands". I agree but wasn't sure what it was I understood.

"Sometimes I see things now. Maybe the closer a person gets to dying the more they can communicate with spirits, I saw something about you". He looked serious as he continued to speak, unaware that my stomach was tying up in knots. I have a dreaded fear of fortune telling or any source that predicts the future.

"It's not really about you, but about your van pool. I saw a lady she is sitting in the back of the driver, not directly in back but the seat behind the seat behind the driver. The lady is wearing yellow; she is scared and angry. The driver is another women, she is wearing red and is making the lady in yellow angry and frightened". It was not much and I thought it was peculiar that he told me what he did. Just to play along with him I said,

"Bob if you see my van pool tell me where my umbrella is, I can't find it".

"It is wedged between the seat and the tire well the man that sits behind you doesn't know that it is there". Several days later, Mary was driving the van, she is a very fast but good driver. She likes to scare people and will swerve when there is nothing in the way. I believe that Mary is an unhappy and angry person and if she can irritate and anger other people she does, maybe trying to relieve some of her own frustrations.

Mary slams on the breaks too hard for no good reason and Betty yells at her to be careful and slow down. This is sort of an everyday occurrence on the van, so everyone else goes back to sleep, because of my brother's prediction, I look over at Betty and see her raise her hand to her head in exasperation. As she raises her hand, I see the yellow sleeve of her blouse peeking out from under her sweater. I shrug off the incident, giving it only a second thought because it was so close to my brother's prediction. When it was my turn to vacate the van, I went to the seat behind me and reached under the seat next to the tire well and removed my umbrella.

CHAPTER 5

I went to see Bob, he was on his last breath. I was able to talk to him the day before but now he appeared to be in a catatonic state. He wasn't sleeping, just laid with his eyes open not responding or recognizing us as we stood by his bedside. That night I woke up out of a troubled sleep with an idea. I remembered what my dad said when he was having his stroke. He was there but everyone thought his brain was gone. My brother was somewhere still and I was determined to find him or at least communicate with him one last time. I desperately wanted him to know I was with him. I believed he needed to know he was not alone, when he left this earth and entered into the next life. I was at Wal-Mart the next morning before the doors opened. I bought a CD player and some of his favorite oldies. One was, I forget exactly how it goes "Jeremiah was a bull frog he was a good friend of mine". Also, we both loved bag pipes so I looked for Irish songs with bagpipes. I found old Irish pub songs; they would have to do. My children and I went over to the hospital. My mom who was faithfully vigilant, at my brother's bedside, was with him when he went home to Jesus. Like I said I wanted this music to let him know I was with him. I know he heard it because when I would take it away, his lips would form a pout sort of like what I see in my grandson's face when I take his favorite toy away.

The night Bob passed away, I was standing by the microwave smoking a cigarette, I am actually not a smoker and only smoke when I drink beer, or on rare occasions, I was drinking a beer and smoking a cigarette and thinking about Bob. I had my hand lightly resting on the cigarette package when I had the sensation that it moved, I know this sounds really questionable but I thought in my head, "If you are Bob and in the cigarette package go to the microwave, if not go to the toaster". The package moved in the direction of the microwave. I ran and got my mom and said,

"Mom, Bob is here he is in my cigarette package". She was still in a state of shock and mentally and emotionally exhausted from the ordeal of losing Bob, because she seemed to go along with the idea that Bob was in the cigarette

43

package. We hurriedly made a make shift wee gee board and put a crystal glass in the middle of it. Bob do you have a message for us?

"I love you he spelled out, you are my sister, quit smoking". I can't remember what else he said, he told my mom he loved her. I know we asked if he was happy and where he was and he seemed too get confused.

I called Hamdi to tell him my brother passed, he said.

"He felt you and loved you. He was tired of pretending everything was okay and making other people smile, he could not on this earth tell anyone how unhappy and alone he felt. He was the one that needed help, but he believed his job on earth was to help other people and always make them smile. He heard the music, he thought you were mad at him but when he heard the music he knew you loved him. "Bob always said he was the doctor and not the patient". Hamdi did not know my brother very well or would he have known how he was feeling. Bob had recently told me it was hard for him to make people laugh anymore, he always felt he had to entertain, sort of like Hamdi himself. I always believed they were sort of kindred spirits connected to me. I was alarmed because I had not told Hamdi about the music.

As the months passed into summer, I had my brother with me. There is a movie "What Dreams May come", the mom is sitting at a table and her dead husband (Robin Williams) writes through her pencil. This is how Bob started communicating with me. When I saw the movie I thought it was eerie, because that was exactly how it happens. Our communication progressed further with me being able to hold my finger on a surface and he would spell out his dialog. It was kind of neat, I had a captive audience. He went camping with me. If I had a problem I discussed it with him, he gave me advice, it was just like talking to Bob on earth. He did not know everything like you would think a spirit would. He had the same poor money sense he did when he was alive. I know this all sounds weird. One afternoon I was sitting in a chair with my thirteen year old daughter Jenny lying on the couch. Bob spelled out on my leg, "I am going to touch Jenny", "don't you dare you'll scare her". I thought back. He wrote back," I love her very much, she loves me, she is pure". Jenny opened her eyes and said, "Mom I felt something strange like someone touched my hand".

"Honey, sometimes your nerve endings can play tricks on you, or it must be the way you're lying on your hand, it must have gone to sleep". She must have bought my explanation because she turned around and closed her eyes.

I could make Bob come whenever I wanted, but now he started going away and I couldn't feel him. I guess you might say I wished him back. It's kind of hard to explain but it's more like willing him back. He didn't want me to call to him, sometimes he wouldn't come. It was like I couldn't reach him. When I did his message was always, "take care of mom".

He came to me very strong one day and said "Dad, needs your help", I was shocked. I thought if there is a higher heaven my dad would be there. I got the impression that my brother had found my dad and he wasn't in the highest heaven, I believed he would be in, he was with Bob and apparently needed help. My instinct was to pray for him. I called my sister, and my mom. We have to go to church and pray for Dad, Bob say's he needs help. My sister has a high level of spiritualism herself she decided that my brother and dad were channeling through me. These are some of the messages I got.

- Want you to be happy one day I'll see you in heaven but, I must be born again to get there. One on earth is okay, but in heaven no. You will remember never alone again.
- Brother Bob loves you Colleen, remember me always, I am happy to go to God I say, Robert Jones gone fishing.
- He draws me a flower and writes "Flower for you, red is love, Green is heaven and Blue is God".
- You are Red and Blue one on earth, Mom is Red and Blue one on earth. Remember me mom, baby boy is back on earth, okay to have one God on earth. Bob is baby on earth, Bob is one in heaven Bob is never one again. Bob is happy to be Bob on

earth again be one on earth okay never be one in heaven.

- Bob's message to his daughter Anne: I love you and you are special to me. Money doesn't mean popo. No man can win love, money kills. You are liking it too much. People make money, not God very dangerous. We are love. Love Robert Jones your father. You are important to me, don't value water because love isn't water. You can value man waters because it brings life. Make me happy know yourself.
- My dad wants to write to my mom he calls her Mary, people don't know how much I love them. Mary be happy, you are upset because you are good. Mary I want to make you happy. You are nice because you love me, you are not mad at me.
- My brother talking to my sister Eileen, "Steve has pie you have lemonade". Eileen said this was an inside joke between the two of them.

Bob would tell her to make him a lemon pie and she could have lemonade.

- There is a circle with an R in the middle. The writing is big, "Jennifer is a beautiful girl. She loves like she forgives, she is nice. She loves God. "Protect you, you are love. You are young and innocent. Colleen and God will worry no evil in jenny".

- From my Dad to my sister: "Eileen, look to yourself to love me because I am your dad you are very special to me. You know he loves you, you are good".

- Bob to his first wife Cathy: "Cathy only woman I loved you are special to me make me happy if you need me, talk to me will need your hand".

- Bob to me: Look at no evil look feel and say enough evil on earth, because only dark for earth ways.

The last thing my brother wrote me is:

MEMORY IS LOVE.

LOVE IS ETERNITY,

REMEMBER ME,

ROBERT JONES GONE FISHING

There was a sweet sadness when he finally left. It was like losing him all over again, the saving grace was at least, I knew he was now happy. I still feel him at Christmas and on his birthday. If I try to contact him, I get what I call a recording. Actually it's like a mantra "Stay at home with your children and don't eat food fat".

The last vision I had filled me with hope. I saw a mass, it is gray, and almost cloud like the mass is feelings. It is my feeling. A big chunk of the mass is ripped away. The pain is devastating, the mass is all of the love I have and have ever known. The part that is ripped away is my brother. I have lost him he is gone. The pain is overwhelming as pieces of the mass disappear all that I am and what I have known is lost. There is a transition I can't see it or feel it, but I am aware that I have passed from one place to another. The mass is resurrected, as all of the pieces are put back together it is happiness, it is love and the incredible feeling of joy is extremely overwhelming. For all is lost and all is gained, when we return to hence we came.

Epilog

I wrote a series of poems to depict the knowledge I have learned for this experience.

POEM ONE

As you gaze upon this beautiful face,

The silent tears you can't erase,

Her eyes aglow with glistening tears,

Weep and weep for all the lost years,

Years filled with strife and hate for a power that doesn't rate,

Don't let greed decide your fate,

Stop and listen before it's too late,

You are me and I am you,

Whether you're white, Catholic or Jew.

POEM TWO

God's little angel she sees a vision of families torn apart because of one division,

As she cries she asks a question,

How can you face your enemy when he or she is part of me,

Be grateful, be glad for all you've had,

Because if you lose it, it's going to be bad,

Treat your neighbor as your kin even if they get under your skin,

For in eternity we're all but one, be kind, be loving, be forgiving, be love if you want to come,

Still inside you feel beautiful,

Still inside you feel young,

But the deterioration in the mirror you can't hide,

What's on the outside.

At a glance in the depth of our own eyes you can become mesmerized by silent tears,

But have no fear the end will never come,

Memory is love,

Love is eternity,

Remember me,

Robert Jones Gone Fishing.

POEM THREE

One little angel sheds a tear,

For a gentle soul that is no longer near,

At least for one brief moment there was a song,

From the lips of all that was wrong,

From a different harmony was an energy that laughed a lot,

Confused by an internal plot,

Destiny is bitter,

Destiny is sweet,

Tomorrow we'll meet,

Love is eternal,

Not all see the beauty of a tree,

Left alone to stand so tall,

With the fleeting breath of nature to caress it's leaves,

He left it part of me,

Never one on earth,

One in eternity,

For two good girls he left behind,

These two are not lost,

Because Robert Jones is the boss in heaven as he thought he was on earth.

POEM 4 (This poem was written for my Mom)

The clock strikes the hour of joy,

For in her womb is a new magnificent baby boy,

The hour strikes the hour of meaning when reason is developed in the wanderlust being,

The hour strikes through the hours of a life span,

When her son becomes a man,

The clock strikes the hours of agonizing sorrow,

When her son sees no tomorrow,

Left behind are clocks that chime with only the memories of time,

Time is an enemy,

Time is a friend,

Filled with hope and joy,

Time brings love that never ends.

Book 2: Little Feather

EPILOGUE

In Oct. of 2007, a guilty verdict came down for young Shawn Khalifa, he had just turned 15 years old, when a crime was committed that changed his young life. The courtroom was at a standstill shallow breaths could be heard as the verdict was read. The jury had tears streaming down their faces this is not the verdict that they wanted. The jury knew the decision was not right just hours before their final decision, the jury asked the judge for a lesser charge.

Shawn was convicted of the Felony Murder Rule. It was clearly known and understood by the Judge and DA that Shawn had nothing to do with taking another's life. He is not believed to be a murder, but he will suffer consequences greater than many who have intentionally murdered another human being.

He is the kid next door, referred to as leave it to Beaver in the DA's opening statements; he is your son, your brother, nephew, best friend, grandson, a person who would take an insect outside and let it go rather than kill it. He was known for his kindness, the amount of love and respect he has for his family admired by many. He is remembered as the little brother of the neighborhood, always riding his bike when his mother arrived home, the thing his mother misses most is his, "Mom what's for supper".

As the Christmas season came to an end that year no one could have guessed what horror was in store for the Khalifa family. The night before Shawn's footsteps were heard clumping up the stairs as usual, as he had a group hug with his mom and sister before bed. The next night he was taken away in a squad car for life.

Shawn and his family are victims of the Felony Murder Rule. Many hearts were broken the day the judge ruled. Shawn with tears streaming down his face vowed in his statements to the court, that he would again be with his mom for Christmas. He pleaded for his innocent young life. The judge gave him the harshest sentence, which is mandatory in the Felony Murder Rule. When Shawn was convicted his only concern was for his mother. It is up to you the people of America to educate yourselves about the ruling and help the many families in the same desperate circumstances as the Khalifa family; the intent is to abolish or modify the rule. This ruling is barbaric in nature and is mentally killing our youth, the bible states, "suffer the children" and that is what is happening because of this ruling. When it was voted in, the persons who voted were not fully aware of the ramifications and ill effect, it has created. Search the web for the Felony Murder

Rule and educate yourself on the repercussions of this ruling and its unconstitutional nature.

I have personally watched many cases where the young innocent victims are subjected to devastating horrors. There are many tortures and cruelties caused by the ruling. As in Shawn's case one minute he is a normal young kid in the next he is ripped form the shelter of his loving home and institutionalized for years, why because he could not control the actions of others. Shawn is not a gang member; he was an asset to society. Please read and digest the following and please contact your government representatives to aid the parents, family and friends of these innocent young victims. There is a high probability this could happen to you.

Murder Felony Rule

The American public is not fully aware of the repercussions of this rule. The fight against gangs and drugs is a war, which has escalated with untold consequences. The intent is to stop the violence and prosecute the offenders to the fullest degree. In all reality there are so many shades of grey to this ruling that it has far more disadvantages then advantages.

Is this working for us? The answer is no; the war against violent teenage crimes and gangs is escalating. The problems are far more out of control and have grown on an upward spiral since this rule was put into place. Prison is a breeding ground for gangs and gang life styles. By placing the innocent victims of Murder Felony Rule in the prison environment, you are in essence throwing them to the lions.

Stop to consider whom we are fighting; **the youth of America**, they are our future. You take a young man, admittedly society's enemy and you put a face on him; he is your brother, my son, your son, in most cases the much beloved youth of America. In so many incidences these kids are not monsters, they were in **the wrong place at the wrong time.** They become victims themselves, their constitutional rights have been stripped from them.

The facts of this rule are hidden in its agenda to use it as a tool in this fight. It has become out of control leaving many victims in its path. The mental cruelty and anguish the youth and their family experience during DO process is unbelievable. Society is taking vital young persons and raping them of their youth, future and mental well-being.

Reference Murder Felony on the Internet and you will find Janet Berger and the Brandon Hein story. Now you have young Shawn Khalifa barely 15 at the time of the crime. He and a friend saw two older youths enter an elderly man's house. They looked in a window to spy on the other two youths and now Shawn has been sentenced to 25 years to life. There are numerous horror stories and persons affected by the tragedy of the murder felony rule; this is growing into an epidemic of numerous proportions. The innocent found guilty by being in the wrong place at the wrong time or by association. In Shawn's case there was no evidence against him, he was found guilty by circumstantial evidence, fabricated by the prosecution.

There is no question of innocence. The reality is that the person is guilty until found guilty. The experience of the DA, who is merely striving for a win, far exceeds the abilities of the general population and especially the young to fight back. Typically the defendants are arrested as a group and no matter what their degree of involvement is they are treated as one. There may be a deal offered to one of the defendants who is rewarded for lying by having his sentence reduced. There is no defense, someone has died and all parties are equally guilty.

- The prosecution can use The Murder Felony Rule as a short cut to justice.

    A. The law relieves prosecutors of the burden of proving intent to kill, thereby making their cases much easier to win.

    B. Because there are only three options for sentencing (Life, life without parole and death), the law can cause grossly disproportionate sentencing, depending on the circumstances of each individual case. This wins prosecutors greater convictions when the sentences may not be at all appropriate.

MURDER FELONY RULE IS UNCONSTITUTIONAL:

A. It does not presume innocence to the first-degree murder charge. If convicted of the underlying felony, the defendant is automatically also guilty of first-degree murder. There is no defense possible against the first-degree murder charge by itself.

B. In some cases it violates the Eighth Amendment: cruel and unusual punishment, grossly disproportionate to the crime(s) actually committed.

C. It holds unequally involved parties equally

accountable and punishable. Again, cruel and unusual punishment if the punishments do not fit each individual's part in the crime.

D. It denies due process on the first-degree murder charge - a violation of the Fifth Amendment. It is not possible, for instance, to plead innocent to the charge of first-degree murder while pleading guilty to the underlying felony. The underlying felony and the first-degree murder charge are bound together and cannot be separated.

COMMENTS

DECLARATIONS OF INTENT:

The world needs change:

1. *The youth of America are being sacrificed and tortured for circumstances they cannot control.*

2. *In Riverside County and under the Felony Murder Rule there are no second chances or rehabilitation; for young minds not fully formed to the potential of maturity, warranted for such severity.*

3. *This barbaric practice is costing the public millions of tax dollars to house the innocent young victims of Murder Felony Rule.*

FACTS

- The Felony Murder Rule is not fair, that is why all of the other countries have abolished it.

- In the US members of our congress must abolish the law; but they don't want to do that because they may be accused of being soft on crime.

- The DA uses the Felony Murder rule as a weapon to extort, it is a means of black male and turning one defendant against another. It's a means of manipulating them by promising manslaughter instead of prison for life.

- The DA essentially does not have to prove their case, they can short cut or super vent the system by streamlining due diligence.

- The cases are grossly misapplied, accelerator and lumped together to save the State money.

- It is offensive to the principle innocent until proven guilty; it is an insult to due process and has nothing to do with justice.

- It is over extended when direct filing and trying multiple juveniles leaving them with no defense.

I always believed in the system and that it was put in place to protect the innocent, I am sure this stems from watching too much TV. The bad guy always got caught and the good guy always is

set free. Tell the truth and all will be fine. What a naïve stupid woman I was.

CHAPTER I

This is for you Shawn: I met Hamdi Khalifa in a bar called the Whistle Stop, actually it was located just across the street from the home I now live in. It was love at first sight. He was remarkably the most brilliant humane being I had ever met. Later I would learn he spoke 5-6 languages, and I am not sure if there was an instrument he could not play. He made me laugh, and entertained me. The only advice I can give after the experience of falling in love and living with a person because they made you laugh and entertained you; is that it may not be the wisest thing a person can do. Those who were close to the family always say something like this,

"We cannot take advice from you after all you married Hamdi Khalifa". There really is no defense for him, all I can say is everyone has their bad and good side. Hamdi's bad side was pretty bad, but his good side was remarkable, he was the kind of hero that books are written about. Sadly enough he did not love himself as I loved him. He had a death wish and was self-destructive; you will find this quality in persons with addictive personalities.

His good side was hidden, I loved being with him and enjoyed our secret moments together most of all I loved watching him love our children. He gave me blessings beyond what I could ever imagine in life; he gave me two brilliant and beautiful children. May you R.I.P. Hamdi Khalifa as you watch down from heaven while I share Shawn's story, thank you for loving me and sharing in our blessings.

Where to start; my son was born just before Thanksgiving, his sister liked to tell him she was planned and he was a mistake. The truth being that I honestly thought I was going through the change of life, when the reality hit me I was pregnant at 42 years old. Being of Irish descent a cold beer after spending a hard day at work; was my reward. The day I reached in the refrigerator and went to take out a beer and my stomach did a summer salt, I knew I was pregnant. When I was pregnant with my first child any thought of alcohol was irritating to me.

My son was so very cute; I can still hear his little feet as they scurried up the stairs;

"Mom there is a sale garage", he would yell excitedly". There were other mom's in the neighborhood and when their kids out grew their toys and clothes, they would pass them down. He had this cute little lisp and would lament, "Arnold Schwarzenegger is the buffest guy in the whole wide warrrld. Ironically the man he so admired at such a young age would be the same man I would write to over and over again to save my young son's life, this was of no avail, I got a form letter back talking about Three Strikes, they did not even have a form letter for Felony Murder, as it relates to juveniles.

Shawn was fostered by my brother, he came to stay with us his last years of life. Shawn whom he called Little Feather was inseparable from him, I can still see them sitting on the couch exactly in the same position. Shawn could play poker before he learned his numbers; I would come home from work and find them in a hard and fast game of rain drop race. They would pick a rain drop as it slid down the window and race them; they were betting pretzels and it was apparent by Shawn's pile that he was the winner.

One day at work when Shawn had just started kindergarten; I got this strong urge to call his school; a mothers intuition is strong and I became increasingly alarmed, when each time I would call the school, they would hang up on me. I was told due to technical difficulties they could not insure that Shawn was in his class room and I would have to call back, this is after they hung up on my numerous times. Several hours later I got a call back saying that they had found Shawn in another school apparently he had been put on the wrong bus in the morning. Luckily he found an older kid from across the street that went to the school and he took him under his wings until he could be shuttled to the right school.

A mothers instinct is strong I remember sitting with Shawn on the stairs of our house and getting a strong feeling that Shawn would be imprisoned. I shook the thought from my head as I looked into the innocent eyes of my beautiful son and I knew instinctively that this was true. I did not question the realization; I just said to myself that what would be, would be and I would deal with this worry when the reality came to fruition. I had enough on my plate and did not have room for any more; at the time Shawn was about 3 years old.

The city of Perris back in the day was a place a person passed through to get to some where else. My dad had been stationed in 29 Palms and we would visit friends and on the way, we would pass through the sleepy little town, it appeared to be depressed and hot, I was only 9 years old at the time but it did not look like a very nice place to live to me. In 1987 it became one of the last hopes for affordable housing in Southern California. I visited the town and was amazed at the transformation. There were beautiful big houses the kind I could only dream about, at fractions of the cost of Orange County. I had been living in Venice beach a good place to visit but if you had kids, forget it, we found out it was called ghost town by the police. They would not deliver pizzas in our neighborhood after sundown; it was not unusual to have swat teams running through the back yards at night. We had bars on the windows and the front door was barricaded.

Perris looked like a paradise compared to this environment. The average families from LA and Orange County started to invest in Perris. The sacrifice was high because the commute was 109 miles one way to my place of employment, but the price of homes was phenomenally low, $400 a month for a 1600 square foot home.

Mothers were pregnant, kids were young, and on weekends there were families moving in, we actually got to watch our homes being built. The neighborhood offered hope, safety and happiness. My brother used to call it a high priced Ghetto. This would prove to be right on the nose, but at the time I was mortally offended by his comments.

All was not as it appeared to be on the surface. The neighborhood would go on weekend binges with the adults fighting and breaking bottles over each other's backs, while I would keep the kids at my house in the guise of a slumber party. They would watch movies, eat popcorn and crash out on the floor, one such night a father broke down his front door and picked up the infant from his crib and started jumping back yard fences. The swat team came to my front door shining lights at the sleeping kids, examining the property for the missing dad.

The neighbors would open their garage doors putting out the ice cooler full of beer early in the morning. They would watch the kids play in the street monitoring their activities until they would pass out drunk, sleep it off and get up and start drinking all over again. There was a lot of drinking going on before the demise of Perris California. It was not unusual for me to have a few extra kids Christmas Eve; their moms in drunken stupors unable to provide any gifts from

Santa. My daughter and I rushed out to any store open 24 hours buying and wrapping presents, so the kids would have something to open in the morning. One of Shawn's best friends watched his dad, who he idolized, puke pure blood from cirrhosis of the liver before his dad died, calling 911 in an attempt to save him. He told us that he slept with his dad and his dad's girlfriend and they'd would have oral sex in the same bed. The kid was too young to know what Oral sex was.

Anyway as the years passed Perris did not prove to be the family friendly town I believed it would be. I would arrange for weekend camp outs and away we would go with at least half of the kids from the neighborhood. We would pack up and go to the lake and have a great time. I grew to love these misguided kids and appreciated the opportunity to bring some joy and fun to their lives. There were so many, some needy and other just a delight to share in their humor, even under some of these ominous circumstances.

Jenny and Shawn had a humor all of their own; they sort of reminded me of me and my brother; there is a certain laugh they have and when I hear it I know that it can't be good. I remember hearing this laugh the first time from my young Jenny, she was about 7 years old and I was walking around the garage and became curious about the gleeful giggles of my sweet little darling girl. As I rounded the corner I heard,

"Eat the candy Shawny, yumm it is so good". There was my little butter ball holding a piece of dog crap in one hand as it approached his mouth, I screamed and grabbed at the disgusting morsel. Jenny was the ideal daughter; she was smart, funny, and helpful, the best shopping buddy a mom could ask for. If it weren't for Jenny I definitely would not have survived the ordeals that would occur in the future.

Shawn loved his big sister and emulated her she would think up some pretty crafty but sometimes now too funny pranks. Who would know she would grow into a pillar of the community and would become an accomplished motivational speaker and health educator, the pride I feel watching her is one of my greatest pleasures. When I look at the beautiful cherub face of my grandson I see both Jenny and Shawn; and then I see the twinkle in his eyes and he gives the same laugh I so remember. Oh Jenny watch out the mothers curse is upon you. Anyway, Jenny wrapped up a Kotex with catsup on it and had Shawn put it on the neighbors door step and ring the bell and run. That is how the infamous office Guzman showed up on our door step.

The joy of my life is to see these two together I love the way their minds work and enjoy their interaction, although they both outgrew me years ago. My mom had 4 boys, my sister and I were the oldest, and the youngest brothers are 10 and 16 years younger than we are. I remember a day when my brother Steve was sitting next to me and I was playing with our baby brother Mark.

He said, "I worry about you Colleen, who are you going to play with when we all grow up"? I will have my own kids, which I did and eventually they grew up too. So now I am playing with my grandson. Life is really great.

As the years passed Shawn had a maturity that was wise beyond his young years. After his uncle passed he took on the role of the male figure in the household. When he was 10, a family down the street was in dire straits. They had two kids, one just an infant. When I found out they could not afford groceries I split my grocery list up and bought one for me and one for them. I bought cheaper cuts of meat and had a very strict budget in order to make my own ends meet, so I included for them the staples I could provide, and after receiving my package, they told me that they preferred boneless, skinless chicken breasts and a higher grade of grape jelly, it set me a back and when I was told by my neighbor across the street that they were telling others that they were planning on moving in with me when they finally were evicted, I said,

"No way, this was not true". I always thought that as long as I could provide a roof, no family or friends of mine would go homeless. Life teaches cruel realities, I quickly learned that being an enabler will get your house and family abused.

As reality has it when they parked their car in my driveway with an infant saying they planned on living there; I opened my door to them. It was a struggle with the additional family in the house. I expected them to get on their feet within a month and when the third month was approaching, and none of the prospects panned out; Shawn sat them

down and had a talk. He basically gave them a
month to move, and asked them to leave the house.
I was so proud of him but at the same time felt
inadequate because he was my strength, where I
was weak. They moved into an apartment quite
easily and I knew the comfort of my home and free
food was no motivation to make them leave on
their own, it took Shawn's talk and reasoning.

The neighborhood started to change and if
you can imagine not for the better. The people
across the street moved. Unknown to me the
families who had originally moved in had not paid
their mortgages for several years they were all
living there mortgage free, so a lot of the property
had gone back to the bank. I paid 90K for my
home it went up to 170K and then plummeted to
60K, in the 90's. The demographics of the
neighborhood changed drastically. The new
neighbors were a family of 4, I would see the dad
outside listening to music and would casually say

hi, but I did not know the family. One day I did not see the dad and a lot of people were coming and going, later I found out he had been car jacked and murdered. Shawn knew a young father in the next neighborhood who had been shot down on the corner of his street. Windows were broken, there was graffiti and ill taken care of houses and yards everywhere, the transformation was sad and disappointing. I started looking for a new job out of state.

The older kids would walk the younger kids to school in a group to insure their safety. Shawn grew from a younger kid to an older kid, as the kids grew older and phased out. He was learning to survive on the streets. In the school system the girls endured better than the boy's. Eventually I put Shawn into a Christian school where he began to thrive, catching up and raising his grades.

CHAPTER 2

I arrived home from work on a Friday about 4:00 and as was our habit I would pick up the kids and we would go out for dinner. When I pulled up to the house Shawn was in front with his friend Ernesto. Shawn wanted to go to Ernesto's house and asked me to bring him home something for dinner. I said no problem as he headed down the street. Jenny, her friend Stephanie and I headed off to our favorite Mexican restaurant in town. It was owned by the town Mayor and we frequented there often. As dinner was finishing I got a phone call the alarm had gone off at home. I was not worried because the dogs would jump on the back slider and trigger the alarm, so I was figuring it was a false alarm. When we pulled up to the house it was like a movie, there were police cars pulled up to the house in different directions. My first thoughts were of Shawn and his safety; I immediately envisioned him dead in the house.

When we entered, they ordered us to the couch, one detective wanted to know where Shawn was at. I noticed the house was damaged severely, the front door and walls broken down. Immediate relief set in as I realized Shawn was not in the house.

"He's at his friend's house", I answered.

"You lead us to the house", one of the detectives told me. I could see Jenny on the couch crying with her friend, another detective was watching them not letting them up. There were cops all over the place pulling out our things and going through them. When I stepped outside of the door one of the Detectives said, "How does it feel to have a son who is a murder"? That was ridiculous to me, Shawn would have me let spiders outside of the house without killing them. He never would hurt another person, it was so ludicrous that not for a minute did I believe the words I was hearing.

"You don't seem surprised, is it because you expected this of your son"?

"No it is because I am in shock and don't believe a word you are saying".

Unbeknownst to all of us, the conversations I was having and future conversations at Ernesto's house were being recorded. On the stand when I recounted the events of the night as they unfolded the judge would state,

"Colleen Khalifa, the mother of Shawn is the only one telling the truth, this was unusual because the mother is the last person I would believe". The detectives lied over and over again denying the events as I told them. My saving grace was that the recordings, the detective had taken of the actual events were released to the court which proved my accounting to be truthful.

The cops broke into Ernesto's house with women and children screaming and crying, they got Shawn and Ernesto out of the bedroom and sat them on the cold pavement outside. The sister demanded a search warrant, as they were searching the house and tearing up Ernesto's bed room. They did find a pipe and marijuana in Shawn's jacket pocket. These items were found the next morning thrown on our front lawn by Mark Shawn's alleged accomplice. It is a mystery to me why they were thrown in our front yard, maybe because they were going to question a 15 year old kid who might not be lucid.

Ernesto kept begging to go to the bathroom and they would not let him. He was gyrating in pain by the time he was allowed to get up. I told Shawn much to my dismay, tell them what you know, I am coming with you. They took pictures of Shawn and put him in cuffs and into the police car.

"Where are you taking him", I asked, "I am going to follow".

"They told me I was not allowed to be present when they questioned him and that they would call when I could pick him up". I waited for hours and no one called me so I decided it was not right for a kid to be questioned without the accompaniment of a parent and went to the station. Shawn had already been arrested and taken away to Juvenile hall. The detectives pulled me and Jenny into a room that had a picture of our house hanging on the wall.

"Your son Mrs. Khalifa has been arrested for murder. A man named Mr. Love was beaten to death in his home during a home invasion robbery gone bad. Shawn admitted to being in the house at the time of the murder, him and his friend Mark. Don't fuck this up for us". I instinctively knew they were lying. I just kept thinking to myself my baby was alone and had not had his dinner, he must be so tired, hungry and scared, I was beside myself. Later when listening to the tapes from the interrogation I discovered not only did Shawn not admit to being in the house but he did not know anything about Mr. Love until they told him at the station during questioning, he had no idea Mr. Love had been murdered, yet he was arrested for this murder.

Earlier after they had taken Shawn to the station for questioning I went home to find Jenny still in tears, they took each one of us into different rooms. Jenny had been home with Shawn the day of the crime and was the only real witness. They had my testimony recorded but conveniently did not have Jenny's in the discovery. Her statements would have impeached Mark and proved him to be a liar.

Mr. Love had been murdered on Tuesday his body was not discovered until Thursday. During my questioning I did not know this and was conveying what I had remembered about Thursday night, which were not accurate for the night of the crime. I remember the night of the crime so vividly each detail is ingrained in my head forever.

During the day on Tuesday, the day the crime actually happened the kids were driving me crazy at work. Mark Gardner came over in the morning a friend of Shawn's. Jenny stayed home from College and was being bothered by Shawn and Mark. Shawn was being home schooled and his daily routine was to complete his studies in the morning, when I got home from work I would work with him at night. I had his curriculum and monitored it daily. Shawn had just barely turned 15, and was responsible enough to be counted on to do his studies daily. He was not allowed to have visitors until they were complete. Jenny called and told me to kick Mark out. Shawn had brought his sister a surprise Sims video game the weekend before and she wanted to play it but Mark and Shawn were hogging the game system.

I said "Put Shawn on the phone, Mark has to go home and you have to do your school work", I directed. He retaliated by saying,

"Mark is not stopping me from doing school work, I am almost done, Jenny just wants to play her game, I promise that I will finish my work please don't make Mark go home". I relented and let Mark stay at the house. He had some real issues with his dad and was kicked out of the house. I knew he had his shoes stolen and was beaten up several days before. He was staying at the house of one of Jenny's church members and was according to him abused and neglected by his father. His girlfriend was the daughter of the mom who had taken him in. I kept getting phone calls throughout the day from Jenny complaining about Mark and Shawn. One of my co-workers is a personal friend of mine and when I had to attend a meeting she fielded the calls and should have been a witness along with Jenny at trial.

Mark was at our house all day. This was opposite of the story he told the detectives about his actions the day of the crime. He said he was at his girlfriends all day taking the bus home he passed our house at 9 O'clock at night, met with Shawn and the youths that beat the elderly man to death, planned the robbery in our front yard and then walked up the street as a gang. The crime occurred at 7:00 pm, Mark stated he did not get to our house until 9:00 pm.

When I got home that night Jenny, Mark and Shawn were still playing the new video game. I had to go to Wal-Mart to get a new house phone, Shawn and Mark had broken the phone a few days before. I went to the store and bought the phone it was about 4:30 in the afternoon. Jenny and I went to a drive through for dinner on the way home. I got Shawn his favorite chicken nuggets and Mark a cheese burger meal. Jenny got a salad with two salad dressings. We got home at 5:30, I had forgotten Shawn's dipping sauce and Jenny would not share hers, so I made ranch sauce with mayonnaise and spices. I remember feeling good because when Shawn tasted the sauce he said to Mark,

"My mom can make anything this sauce is really good". Moms are like that throw them a bone and they glow.

I worked with Shawn for a while on his school work and then started to pick up the house which included taking out the trash. Trash day was the next day. The kids kept playing the video game. At 7:00 Jenny had to attend a church meeting so they all came out of the house together at just before 7:00, as I was filling the trash can I saw the two boys (Shawn and Mark) walk up the street. They were alone, our little pug followed them and I had to chase after him to bring him home. Shawn caught him and walked him back to me. All of this happened with no sight of any other persons. Jenny followed behind them in the car leaving for her meeting.

I take a bath every night at 7:00 because I have to leave the house at 3:30 in the morning, I kept a very strict schedule. I get a bath from 7:00 to approximately 7:20. I go down and check on the kids and then watch TV until 8:00 at which time I fall asleep. This night while I was taking a bath Shawn comes up stairs, he comes into the bathroom, so he was gone approximately 20-30 minutes from the house. He comes into the bathroom wearing the exact same cloths he had left in. I thought he was just checking in to let me know he was home. After I get dressed for bed I went down stairs to check and he was playing the video game. Just before 8:00 he came to my room and wanted to know if he could lay down with me. This was unusual because he had outgrown sleeping with me a long time ago. He started talking to me about an incidence he had witnessed.

"Mom, two guys went into a man's house up the street, I think they were robbing him, Me and Mark tried to look into the window".

"What the hell" I yelled,

" Do you know that if they were robbing the man you could get blamed"? Stay away from those kids and out of other people's yards, I cut him short slightly irritated because if I didn't get enough sleep the morning commute would be torturous. He left my bed and went down stairs only to return again, Shawn was doing the right thing he was telling an adult.

I had been robbed in that neighborhood every other month, in fact my house had been robbed so many times my home owners insurance was cancelled. Shawn returned to my bed and laid there until Jenny got home, once she came in he talked her into sleeping in his room. This was very unusual, I got concerned and went to check on them. Jenny was laying in the top bunk with

Shawn and something was said that should have alarmed me.

"Is Fernando going to come in the night and shoot us? I said,

"That is crazy why would Fernando shoot us? On Thursday the street was roped off with cops up the street. When I asked Shawn what happened he said, a girl that lived at Robert's house up the street, her boyfriend was killed and found in a ravine.

The day after Shawn was arrested Mark kept calling the house. I woke up the morning after he was arrested and got on the phone finding he had been taken to the juvenile hall in Riverside. One time I had a nightmare that Shawn had been run over by a car in the street. I think all moms have these kind of dreams. In the dream my neighbor came running into the house saying,

"Shawn was dead". I woke up, but the nightmare seemed so real it took me a long time to shake it.

This reality was just like the nightmare except it was real and there was no waking up to make it go away. I had to go to the juvenile hall to register to visit Shawn. I moved like a zombie, reality had not set in. At the first visit I stood waiting for the parents to be let into the hall. Tears just kept running down my face there was no controlling them. The sadness I felt was only compounded by what I saw walking through the various levels of the Hall. There was a pungent smell of pine, the floors were cement the walls were gray. The first level I walked through was surreal there were iron doors that had small windows with bars. Through the windows were young, scared, lost eyes staring out. Some of the kids appears to be younger than 12. Babies behind bars, kids sometimes sleep with the light on seeing monsters and ghosts in the darkness, one can only imagine what these kids were feeling and seeing.

Our first visit was in an open area outside in a yard. Shawn was escorted to me and we sat on a bench talking. He told me that Mark and he saw two older kids Fernando and Juan walking up the street. They wanted to buy pot from them, so they decided to find them. They saw JR the kid that lived on the corner and asked him if he had seen where the two had gone. JR hadn't seen them so they continued across the street to Roberts's house. They saw the Castillo brothers in Roberts's front yard. They greeted and talked to them for a while and then they started to walk to Ernesto's house, they crossed the street to the crazy Green house across the street from Mr. Loves house. They stood there for a while deciding what to do, when they saw Fernando and Juan go to Mr. Loves front door. They decided to spy on them with the intention of getting their attention to buy the pot.

They crossed the street hid behind Mr. Love's car creeping into the side yard. They heard Fernando or Juan yelling inside of the house got scared and ran. They knew that if Fernando or Juan knew that they were spying on them at the widow they would beat them up, they were want-to-be's and not of the caliber of the two criminals in the house, and not socially accepted into their peer level.

They got several streets over when Fernando and Juan drove up in a car. They ordered them to get in, which they did because they were scared of the two and did not want to suffer the outcome if they did not obey, Fernando then drove to the stop sign across the street from the neighborhood convenience store called, "Hazit". Juan was in the passenger side, while Fernando was driving the car. Juan pulled out a gun which went off and put a bullet through the bottom left side of the car. Fernando retaliated by shooting Juan, Shawn only heard the explosion of the bullets as he jumped out of the car and ran home. Fernando later told him his only regret was he ran out of bullets before he could shoot Shawn.

I had no idea of the Felony Murder rule and took Shawn statement at face value, reporting the details to the detective when I drove Mark to the police station the night after Shawn was arrested. We heard helicopters and got a call from Katie, Marks girlfriend saying that the police were looking for Mark. He showed up at our door step, and I talked him into letting me take him to the station. He was crying and not auditable during the drive to the station. I remembered the words of the detective to, "Not fuck this up by talking about the details he had given us at the meeting", so I was careful not to give Mark any details. In my mind once Mark told the detectives what happened he and Shawn would be released. I had no idea that Mark had no integrity and would save his own hide by selling Shawn down the River to get a deal. When a person's life is at stake, what level they will stoop to for survival? Lying was the option Mark chose. I have in my possession the interviews at the police station and the detective walked Mark through the process by stating facts, all he did was agree with what he was basically told to say. It was so peculiar at one point when the Detectives told him he could be charged with murder, he started screaming and climbing the walls, the detectives left the room and Mark calmly sat down and started to clean his finger nails. The dramatic change in his behavior was startling. The detectives returned and started questioning him again.

"What were you doing in the house"? They shouted at him.

"I was not in the house", he appeared to get hysterical,

"What was Shawn doing in the house"? They fed him the answers they wanted to hear. He had previously said that he and Shawn were together through the whole ordeal. They would twist his words leading him into the confession they wanted.

During Shawn's interview they told him if he told them what they wanted to hear he could go home, so at the end he started to agree with everything they said. Instead of going home he was arrested and put into a car with Fernando who he was desperately afraid of; during that ride he just agreed with everything Fernando said, he was scared to death of him and wondered why they would put him in harm's way.

After Mark was taken from my car at the police station Jenny and I were told to park and wait until someone came out and talked to us. We waited for what seemed like forever and a detective came out and got us. I recounted what Shawn had told me and he called me a liar and Shawn a murderer. He again told me that Shawn admitted to being in Mr. Loves house, which later I found out was a lie when I listened to the tapes from the interview at the police station.

For months I would visit the Riverside juvenile hall. I would get extreme stress with each visit; walking through the halls to see Shawn was agony, the eyes of the children locked away and forgotten was torturous. Shawn, a kid that was not allowed to spend the night over at other kid's houses, was loved and had group hugs every night was thrown into solitary confinement to the standards of a maximum security prison. He was locked away with his own thoughts for months; His only resort in his mind was to commit suicide to relieve the conditions he was imprisoned in, he tried and failed. I would walk through the halls with dismay and contempt for the stark cruel conditions, crossing a yard with grass knowing that when I walked up the stairs and entered the building, I would see my own young son in pain, lost and scared, I felt an anguish that only a mother can feel.

The first time I saw him shackled in court my heart stopped, I would endure the court appointments checking my blood pressure to insure I did not have to call 911. The levels would go from 200 systolic to 175 diastolic, I knew I had to live through this ordeal to take care of and protect my children. At one point my heart beat was 230 beats a minute and I was hospitalized and diagnosed with, "A fib". The horrible reality was that I had to rely on my daughter to keep going when I was unable to. The ordeal was taking a toll on her, but God bless her she made it through. During the trial I testified and Jenny fielded the day's I was too sick to attend. I knew I had to live and had to take whatever steps necessary to survive. Jenny was my savior it took a noticeable toll on her, but she weathered through it like a real trouper, my most precious darling I will always regret what she was put through.

Diana was Jenny's best friend and part of the family, she had a brother and three sisters. Katie, Marks girlfriend was one of these sisters. Some of the siblings had severe mental problems. Their mom passed away after Mark and Shawn were arrested. Another lesson in life was learned. I wanted to keep the siblings together, so I took them in. Jenny belonged to the Mormon church, the members were good caring people so I should have questioned my decision as I was warned against what I felt was a noble deed. If a person is not a professional they have no right to step in and guarantee, safety and unity when children that are mentally challenged are involved. I don't want to go into the details but will say that the son would hit his head against the wall saying over and over again,

"Fuck my mother, fuck my sister", money was stolen, our beloved dog was missing, and outrageous accusations were made. I would come home from work and Tony would raise his fist to hit me if I asked him to turn his music down. The music was of the category of off color rap, and it blared and pulsated throughout the house as he continued to lament the words,

"Fuck my Mother, Fuck my sister" hitting his head against the wall. When I realized he was a physical threat to me I would call the police and ask for assistance. He would throw things like the TV breaking many items. I took the children to see phycologists on the weekends. At one such session, the phycologist told me that I had made a mistake in bringing the children into my home not only was I in danger but I was also putting my child in danger. They recommended they be put into homes with professionals, who could control and help them.

I contacted the case worker and found that the youngest girl had put in many erroneous reports against her loving mother saying she was on drugs and cared for them poorly. She was accused of abusing them which all that knew the mom would never believe. I could see this pattern transferred to me. The case worker was able to find a home for this young girl that was a better fit for her needs. The new foster mom was seasoned and much better prepared to give the much needed special attention to her. No good deed goes unturned they say and this experience proved that to be right. So the words become Mother love, was not appropriate, I will always regret my decision to take these young needy children in on top of the trials I was already experiencing.

It has been years and I have not been able to finish this book reliving the experiences is still too stressful for me. I have been well for years but find I have to monitor my blood pressure as I force myself to think about how I felt. So in-between my accounting of the events I will relieve tension by inserting some of the facts of the case. I know that there will be a discontinuity to our story but if I want to convey the experience I will need to take this course, with the least damage to my health and wellbeing. I have always been reluctant to relive the pain but that is what has to be done to educate others of the plight of the felony murder ruling and direct filing of youths and it must be done. I know that once I have finished the book it will be equally painful to read and edit. I still to this day pretend when I see a male of Shawn's stature that the person is Shawn and all I have to do is pull over and take him home.

CHAPTER 3

This chapter will include the status of Shawn's case and the facts that lead to his life sentence. I do want to convey my experience at the time of sentencing. The DA and investigating detective lied over and over again throughout the trial. When Shawn was sentenced to 25 years in an adult prison, to life, the DA first turned and gave me a shit eating grim this is the only way to describe it, as he walked past me, the triumph clearly written in his eyes. Who would do that to the mom, clearly grieving? The detective followed with a grin that caused me to grimace to my very soul, there was evil in their eyes, I was told that culpability and innocence was not a factor, and that the experience of the DA in getting a 99% conviction rate was their win at whatever expense.

There were tears in the eyes of the jury as they came down with the only sentence the Judge had given them; although they had asked for a lesser sentence one that more fit the crime. It was apparent that they knew how inappropriate their choice was but their hands were tied. Below are statements made by Harry's Law one episode before it was taken off the air.

This is what I got from Harry's Law show:

- The Felony Murder Rule is not fair, that is why all of the other countries have abolished it.

- In the US members of our congress must abolish the law, but they don't want to do that because they may be accused of being soft on crime.

- The DA uses the Felony Murder rule as a weapon to extort, it is a means of blackmail and turning one defendant against another. It's a means of manipulating them by promising manslaughter instead prison for life.

- The DA essentially does not have to prove their case, they can short cut or super vent the system by streamlining due diligence.

- The cases are grossly misapplied, accelerator and lumped together to save the State money.

- It is offensive to the principle innocent until proven guilty; it is an insult to due process and has nothing to do with justice.

- He Judge has the say if the law is ligament when the law is over reaching oppressive which what the Felony murder rule is one.

- It is over extended when direct filing and trying multiple juveniles leaving them with no defense.

Shawn was the only one tried for the murder of Mr. Love he was the youngest and the least culpable. Mark admitted that he lied on the stand

and that the DA and detectives fed him what to say to get a deal. There was no evidence against Shawn and he was the only person tried for Mr. Loves murder, and the only defendant ordered to pay retribution, to date I am close to paying this 10K off. It was heart breaking to watch as my son sat while the horrific pictures of Mr. Love were displayed. The perception was that he was the monster that committed this gruesome crime.

The DA really knows his stuff, he declared me a liar and the worst enemy of the court, and this was for telling the truth. The sad fact is money talks. The night I graduated high school the son of a dr. executed three fisherman and stole their boat. He parents were wealthy and prominent members of society. He was released after serving 7 years, actually committing the murders. Prison is a huge business in California with the guards making close to 100K a year. In the old day's it was crops that were the main commodity in California, now it is prisons and I truly believe the system is designed to support this.

` A classic book, American Tragedy should be written as the felony murder rule as it relates to juveniles, truly the lost boys. This ruling was designed to curtail crime but at the same time there was no consideration for the young victims that would be the catch 22 of the ruling. These are but a few of the discrepancies of Shawn's trial. As routine has it, Shawn lost all appeals up to the Supreme Court. This is a dissertation written by a Ninth Circuit judge.

FILED

UNITED STATES COURT OF APPEALS

FOR THE NINTH CIRCUIT

FEB 19 2015

MOLLY C. DWYER, CLERK
U.S. COURT OF APPEALS

SHAWN MALONE KHALIFA,	No. 12-56230
Petitioner - Appellant,	D.C. No. 5:10-cv-01446-GAF-PLA
v.	Central District of California, Riverside
BRENDA M. CASH, Warden,	
Respondent - Appellee.	ORDER AMENDING

Before: PREGERSON, TALLMAN, and BEA, Circuit Judges.

The dissent filed on November 25, 2014 is hereby amended.

Khalifa v. Cash, No. 12-56230 (Amended Dissent)

PREGERSON, Circuit Judge, dissenting:

Shawn Khalifa[1] appeals his felony murder conviction arguing his Sixth

Amendment speedy trial rights were violated.

The disposition correctly applied the first *Barker* factor by finding that the

three-and-a-half year delay was "clearly lengthy and thus presumptively

prejudicial." The disposition correctly determined that the second factor was

neutral because most of the delay was caused by Khalifa's co-defendants' requests

for continuances.

Contrary to the disposition I submit that the third factor regarding the

forcefulness of Khalifa's assertion of his speedy trial right was not neutral. A

[1] Khalifa was just two months beyond his fifteenth birthday when the crime occurred. He and Mark Gardner were acting as lookouts for a burglary while two older boys entered the victim's home through the front door. Khalifa allegedly snuck through the backdoor and took a handful of candy from the victim's kitchen. The older boys beat the elderly homeowner to death. Khalifa was found guilty of first degree felony murder and sentenced to twenty-five years to life. Based on Khalifa's limited participation and his status as a juvenile, this sentence appears unusually harsh. As the Supreme Court has found, children like Khalifa lack maturity and have "an underdeveloped sense of responsibility leading to recklessness, impulsivity, and heedless risk-taking." *Miller v. Alabama*, 132 S. Ct. 2455, 2464 (2012). Further, the brain of a fifteen year old is "not yet fully mature in regions and systems related to higher-order executive functions such as impulse control, planning ahead, and risk avoidance." *Id.* at 2464, n.5 (internal citations ommitted).

defendant's assertion of his speedy trial right is "entitled to strong evidentiary

weight in determining whether the defendant is being deprived of the right."

Barker v. Wingo, 407 U.S. 514, 531-32 (1972). Khalifa objected to continuances

on five separate occasions during the eight month period between October 2006

and June 2007. To vindicate his right to a speedy trial he moved to sever his case

from those of his co-defendants. While Khalifa consented to much of the delay,

that consent does not neutralize the fact that he forcefully asserted his speedy trial

rights for eight consecutive months. A delay of eight months on this record is most

likely presumptively prejudicial. *See United States v. Gregory*, 322 F.3d 1157,

1162 n.3 (9th Cir. 2003). This third factor weighs in favor of Khalifa.

Finally, I submit that Khalifa was prejudiced by the eight month delay.

Prejudice should be assessed by considering "the interests of defendants which the

speedy trial right was designed to protect . . . : (i) to prevent oppressive pretrial

incarceration; (ii) to minimize anxiety and concern of the accused; and (iii) to limit

the possibility that the defense will be impaired." *Barker*, 407 U.S. at 532. Here, the disposition does not explicitly touch upon the first two interests. Khalifa was

prejudiced by his pretrial incarceration. He spent over three years in jail awaiting

trial. Khalifa was arrested on January 30, 2004, three days after the crime was

committed and about two months beyond his fifteenth birthday. His trial started on

2

September 17, 2007, a couple months before his nineteenth birthday. In *Barker*,

the Supreme Court determined that "time spent in jail awaiting trial has a

detrimental impact on the individual." *Id.* Khalifa's three-and-a-half year pretrial

incarceration and the anxiety it caused him–a teenager awaiting trial for felony

murder–weigh in favor of finding that Khalifa was prejudiced by the delay.

The delay also impaired, and thus prejudiced, Khalifa's defense because the

The delay also impaired, and thus prejudiced, Khalifa's defense because the only non-biased eyewitnesses, one of whom was Erick Castillo, left the country and moved to Mexico during the delay. *See Id.* at 532 ("If witnesses . . . disappear during a delay, the prejudice is obvious."). Because lengthy delays often cause the loss of exculpatory evidence and testimony, "impairment of one's defense is the most difficult form of speedy trial prejudice to prove." *Doggett v. United States,* 505 U.S. 647, 655 (1992). For this reason, "consideration of prejudice is not limited to the specifically demonstrable." *Id.*

Further, the California Court of Appeal's factual determination that witness Castillo's preliminary hearing testimony was consistent with co-defendant Mark Gardner's testimony was refuted by clear and convincing evidence. Khalifa's appellate brief demonstrated that Castillo's preliminary hearing testimony varied from Gardner's testimony on several points; most notably co-defendant Gardner testified to facts that made him appear less culpable. Gardner testified that he was only in the side yard briefly before waiting in front of the house for Khalifa, whereas witness Castillo saw Khalifa and Gardner leave the side yard together. The jury may have discounted Gardner's account as biased if Castillo had testified at trial because it appears as if Gardner may have twisted the facts to minimize his involvement. The jury might have taken this into consideration when weighing Gardner's credibility. Co-defendant Gardner also portrayed Khalifa as having a more active role in the crime by testifying that Khalifa exited the home only seconds before Rivera and Pena (the men who beat the victim to death), not five to ten minutes before as explained by Castillo. Gardner's version makes it more likely that Khalifa was in the home during the victim's murder, however, Castillo's account presents an issue as to Khalifa's presence during and his knowledge of the killing. Had the jury heard these varied accounts it would have had to weigh the credibility of both witnesses and it is likely there would have been more discussion about co-defendant Gardner's motivations for testifying. Likely, there also would have been a more in-depth consideration of the extent of Khalifa's involvement.

For these reasons, the loss of Castillo as a witness at trial prejudiced Khalifa.

Three of the four Barker factors weigh in Khalifa's favor and support a finding of a violation to his right to a speedy trial under the Sixth Amendment. Therefore, Khalifa's habeas petition should have been granted.

4

The only issue before this panel was whether Khalifa was denied his right to a speedy trial. Before the state courts and the district court, Khalifa challenged the constitutionality of his 25 years to life sentence as unconstitutionally cruel and unusual on account of his age and his relative culpability for the murder. Before our court, Khalifa petitioned for a certificate of appealability challenging the constitutionality of his sentence as cruel and unusual under the Eighth

Amendment, but the motion was denied. **Docket 3**. Even the deputy attorney general in this case acknowledged the harshness of Khalifa's sentence for a kid who went into a house and filled his pockets with candy.

Khalifa played the relatively minor role of lookout during the robbery of an elderly man. Much of the evidence against Khalifa came from Gardner, one of Khalifa's co-defendants who testified for the prosecution in exchange for a lighter sentence. Gardner testified that the night of the offense, he was hanging out with Rivera, Pena, and Khalifa. Khalifa was the youngest at 15 years of age. The group began discussing their need for money and someone suggested robbing an elderly neighbor.

The four boys walked toward the victim's home, Rivera and Pena in front and Gardner and Khalifa following behind. Gardner explained that Rivera and Pena told Gardner and Khalifa to wait outside while Rivera and Pena went up to the victim's front door and entered. Gardner testified that he and Khalifa went through a gate leading to the victim's backyard. Gardner also testified that Khalifa entered the victim's home, was inside the kitchen for a couple minutes, and looked through the kitchen drawers. Khalifa took candy from the victim's kitchen and then left through the back door.

There was no evidence that Khalifa saw the victim being beaten, but the evidence indicates that Khalifa may have heard the victim moan. Khalifa and Gardner then returned to the front of the home. After killing the homeowner, Rivera and Pena came out the front door and drove down the street in the victim's car. Khalifa got in the car at the prompting of Rivera and Pena.

Khalifa was tried and convicted of first degree felony murder in connection with his alleged participation in the burglary and robbery. He was sentenced to 25 years to life, the most severe punishment available for a 15 year old convicted of first degree murder in California. *See* Cal. Penal Code § 190.5. In fact, Khalifa received the same maximum sentence he would have received had he entered through the front door and participated in the killing of the victim.

He had just turned 15 at the time of the crime. He did not kill anyone and there is no evidence that he could have foreseen that the victim would be killed; he entered the victim's kitchen at the rear of the house and took some candy while

6

two older boys robbed and beat the victim in the living room in the front of the house. He was sentenced to 25 years to life.

The Supreme Court's recent decisions tell us that "children are constitutionally different from adults for purposes of sentencing." We also are told by the Court that "when compared to an adult murderer, a juvenile offender who did not kill or intend to kill has a twice diminished moral culpability." *Miller v.*

did not kill or intend to kill has a twice diminished moral culpability." *Miller v. Alabama*, 132 S. Ct. 2455, 2468 (2012) (quoting *Graham v. Florida*, 130 S.Ct. 2011, 2027 (2010)).

Further, "compared to adults, juveniles have a lack of maturity and an underdeveloped sense of responsibility; they are more vulnerable or susceptible to negative influences and outside pressures, including peer pressure; and their characters are not as well formed." *Graham*, 560 U.S. at 68 (internal quotations omitted).

In addition, as Justice Breyer notes in his concurrence in *Miller*, the felony murder rule "traditionally attributes death caused in the course of a felony to all participants who intended to commit the felony, regardless of whether they killed or intended to kill. This rule has been based on the idea of transferred intent; the defendant's intent to commit the felony satisfies the intent to kill required for murder." *Miller*, 132 S.Ct. at 2476 (internal quotations and citations omitted).

Justice Breyer further noted that the "theory of transferring a defendant's intent is premised on the idea that one engaged in a dangerous felony should understand the risk that the victim of the felony could be killed, even by a confederate. Yet the ability to consider the full consequences of a course of action and to adjust one's conduct accordingly is precisely what we know juveniles lack capacity to do effectively." *Id.* (internal citation omitted).

Given Khalifa's age and his minor involvement in the crime, his sentence appears unusually harsh and cruel. I believe that this issue should have been considered.

Despite, this dissertation Shawn was denied an appeal, we then went to the Supreme Court and his appeal was again denied. These are the facts that have not been recognized by the court.

These are the details submitted by his lawyer for the appeal:

STATEMENTOFTHEFACTS Shawn Khalifa was 15 years old when two older boys, Rivera (16 years old) and Pena (18 years old) said they needed money and suggested they might rob an elderly man they knew. (District Court Opinion, 2:26-3:2) The State's only witness against Shawn was his friend Mark Gardner (17 years old) who was also present. Gardner testified that Shawn neither participated in the discussion, agreed, encouraged, nor was asked to participate in the crime. (District Court Opinion, 2:26-3:4) Shawn agreed to walk Gardner home and Rivera and Pena left with them. Shawn and Gardner walked fifteen to twenty feet behind the older boys on their way to Gardner's home. (Opinion, 3:4-8) Directly on the way from Shawn's home to Gardner's home they passed the victim's home. The two older boys told Shawn and Gardner to "wait here," and walked up to the house and walked in the front door, leaving Shawn and Gardner standing on the sidewalk. (Opinion 3:9-14) Gardner testified neither he nor Shawn agreed to act as 'lookouts' or to even stay there. (Opinion 3:12-13) The home of the victim was directly along the path between Shawn's home and Gardner's home - Shawn had not gone out of his way to arrive there. (Opinion, 3:9-10) Shawn and Gardner waited between five and twenty minutes and finally decided to go to the side of the house and look in a window to see what was happening. The window showed the kitchen of the house, but no one was visible. (Opinion3:20-22,3:27-28) Later, Gardner accepted a plea of manslaughter in exchange for testifying that while he and Shawn were standing at the side window, Shawn went around the back of the house. Gardner claimed he then saw Shawn in the kitchen of the house looking through drawers. (Opinion 3:22-26) Although Gardner was watching Shawn the entire time, Gardner never saw Shawn take anything. According to Gardner there were voices from within the house and moments later Shawn came back around the side of the house and indicated they ought to leave. Shawn did not want to talk about what he'd heard. (Opinion 4:1-4, 6-7, 13-14) According to Gardner, Shawn was not carrying anything in his hands, nor did it appear he had anything in his pockets. (Opinion, 4:4-5) Gardner testified that the next day Shawn told him that the older boys had beat the elderly man who lived there, but Shawn said one the older boys told him this, he did not say he saw it. (Opinion,4:23-25) After leaving the scene, Shawn and Gardner continued walking to Gardner's home. Before they reached it, about five minutes after leaving the crime scene, Rivera and Pena drove up to them in a car they had taken from the home. (Opinion, 4:14-15) They told Shawn and Gardner to come with them. Gardner said he was already nearly home, but Shawn climbed in the back seat. The car was later recovered and several foil wrapped chocolate liqueurs were discovered in the backseat. (Opinion5:8-9) Police and the victim's family members testified there were chocolate liqueurs in the kitchen of the victim. (Opinion5:27-6:1) At trial Gardner's testimony against Shawn was allowed because the trial court determined there was corroborating evidence showing Shawn was present. But presence at the scene of a crime is not sufficient to make one guilty of felony murder and the corroborating evidence was testimony of Shawn's mother regarding correspondence from Shawn. But such corroborating evidence specifically lacked any claim Shawn agreed, encouraged, participated or was asked to participate in a robbery or burglary. It lacked any indication Shawn was aware that Rivera and Pena were actually headed to the victim's home when they joined Shawn and Gardner while they were walking Gardner home. They lack any corroboration that Shawn entered the victim's home. Trial court also claimed the presence of chocolate liqueurs in the back seat of the car, where Shawn might have been sitting, corroborates

Gardner's testimony. But Gardner testified he was watching Shawn in the victim's kitchen and at no time did Gardner testify Shawn picked up anything. Gardner also testified specifically that upon leaving the victim's home, Shawn had nothing in his hands or pockets. Shawn was convicted of first degree murder under a felony murder theory, with special circumstances of murder during the commission of a robbery and murder during the commission of a burglary. (Opinion,2:3-10) After trial Shawn, through counsel, filed a direct appeal which the State Appellate Court denied and which the State Supreme Court denied without comment. Shawn subsequently filed pose the same issues in the Federal District Court. The District Court held that the decision of the State court did not contradict nor was it an unreasonable application of Federal law as defined by the US Supreme Court because, (1) an eight-month delay over the continued objections of Shawn's attorney did not amount to a

violation of Shawn's Constitutional right to a
speedy trial because it produced no prejudice, (2)
that Shawn's attorney was not ineffective due to
his failure to ask for jury instructions for the lesser
inclusive offenses because Shawn's attorney's
decision was based upon a tactical decision, (3)
that is wasn't ineffective assistance of counsel not
to object to the trial court instructing the jury that
Shawn's testifying codefendant was an accomplice
"as a matter of law" because it produced no
prejudice,(4) that a reasonable trier of fact could
have found Shawn guilty beyond a reasonable
doubt based upon the evidence, and that (5) that
the sentence of 25 years to life for a 15-yearold,
even taking into account Shawn's relative lack of
culpability, did not constitute cruel and unusual
punishment under the Eighth Amendment to the
US Constitution because the only cases from the
US Supreme Court regarding juveniles and their
relative culpability were "new law" and not
applicable to Shawn. As per the Ninth Circuit's

rule 22-1(d), Shawn Khalifa asks the Ninth Circuit for permission to appeal the District Court's denial of his Habeas Petition.

Issue One: Was petitioner's right to a speedy trial violated by a nine-month delay during which petitioner asked to have his trial severed from his codefendants five times?

The Federal District Court held correctly that, ""The Sixth Amendment guarantees that, [i]n all criminal prosecutions, the accused shall enjoy the right to a speedy ... trial." ... This constitutional guarantee is governed by a flexible four-factor inquiry set forth by the Supreme Court in Barker v. Wingo, 407 US 514 (1972). Under Barker, to determine whether a "speedy trial" violation has occurred, the court must weigh the following: (1) the length of the delay; (2) the reason for the delay; (3) the petitioner's assertion of his right; and (4) prejudice to the petitioner due to the delay. ... No single factor is controlling or necessary; rather, the factors must be considered "together with such other circumstances as may be relevant." (Id. at 533)" (District Court Opinion, 9:24-10:8, citations removed). The Federal District Court used the Baker test to analyze Shawn's claim of a violation of his right to speedy trial. Under the first factor the District Court held that the 43-month delay covering Shawn's entire time from arrest to trial was "presumptively prejudicial." (Dist Court Opinion, 17:12-17) But it also pointed out that that lower courts have generally found delays to be "presumptively prejudicial" when they approach a year. (17:18-19) The delay Shawn actually complained about were the eight months between October17, 2006, and June 19, 2007. Under the second factor the Court then claimed that the second factor was against Shawn. The District Court admitted the relevant question was whether the delay was more the fault of Shawn or the prosecution. (17:21-22) The District Court admitted the eight month delay complained of by Shawn, in which his trial was continued five times over the objections of his counsel and each time for scheduling problems with the other attorneys - and despite the fact the other attorneys were twice ordered by the Trial judge to not make scheduling conflicts (Opinion 18:10-16), was not Shawn's fault and that one of the times was the joint fault of the prosecutor who had scheduled another trial even after being told by the trial judge to make sure there were no more conflicts to delay the trial. The Federal District Court erred in confusing the entire 43 month delay with the 8 months Shawn was delayed between October 17, 2006 and June 19, 2007. The fact Shawn asked for continuances and/or agreed to continuances earlier in the process cannot somehow make the 8 critical months he was delayed not prejudicial. If this is the reasoning then any Shawn who asks for continuances or who accepts requests for continuances, will somehow waive all objections for any and all future unreasonable delays. This cannot be a legitimate interpretation of the meaning or purpose of the

Constitutional protection. The District Court erroneously claimed the completely unrelated continuances were Shawn's fault (at 20:20-21) and therefore the "blame" for the overall delay was neutral.

Clearly Shawn was not to "blame" for the eight months in question, and clearly the prosecutor was partially to blame for these delays. Just as clearly, prior continuances necessary to Shawn for the proper and professional handling of his defense cannot immunize the entire case from challenges for unreasonable delays. As for the third factor, the District Court held that the fact that Shawn's counsel objected to each of the five continuances during this time period was a factor that was "entitled to strong evidentiary weight in determining whether the [petitioner] [was] deprived of the right."(Opinion20:23-21:2) This is telling because the District Court clearly is only talking about the eight months in question, not the entire 43-months between Shawn's arrest and his trial. This is strong evidence even the District Court knows the legitimate interpretation of the test involves the actual eight month delay complained of, not the entire 43 months delay from arrest to trial. And as for the fourth factor, the District Court held that there was no prejudice, despite the fact the District Court claims one of the ways in which prejudice can manifest is "the possibility that the [accused's] defense will be impaired by dimming memories and loss of exculpatory evidence." (Opinion, 21:9-10) The District Court goes on to use the example of the unavailability of witnesses. The District Court accepts that Shawn's five requests for severance based upon delay were denied, but his co-defendant was severed from the trial immediately after the eight month delay (19:16-18) and then the co-defendant was given a deal in which he presented the only testimony against Shawn. The District Court held that the claim Shawn was prejudiced was therefore speculative because he couldn't prove that his codefendant wouldn't have been given a deal earlier if the Court had granted Shawn's request for severance. But this argument turns the question on its head. The fact is that Shawn was not granted severance, his trial was delayed, the police only pressured Shawn's co-defendant into testifying against Shawn in September of 2007. It is actually speculation to say that even if Shawn was allowed to sever his trial and bring it to a jury eleven months prior to the police offering his co-defendant a deal, perhaps his codefendant would have made a deal with police and agreed to testify against Shawn. Shawn only has to show prejudice. His codefendant's deal was in no way related to when Shawn went to trial. All evidence suggests it was related to the police acquisition of incriminating taped evidence against him in September 2007 (Opinion, 19:16-18). The District Court's citation to United States v. Beamon, 992 F.2d 1009 (9th Cir. 1993) (Opinion, 20:3-7) is misplaced. Beamon was a case where the defense was trying to speculate that the police would have made defendant a better deal absent the delay. Trying to guess what the police would and wouldn't have done is speculation. In petition's case he is doing the opposite. We already know what happened and there is no speculation there during the period of delay the police found incriminating evidence against Shawn's codefendant and the co-defendant agreed to testify against petition in return for a deal. It is the State that is trying to speculation as to what Shawn's co-defendant would or would not have done absent the delay. More incredibly, the State is speculating that, for reasons which can't possibly be imagined, Shawn's co-defendant would have agreed to testify against Shawn prior to the discovery of the incriminating tapes. This is not only speculation, but it begs the question, why would Shawn's co-defendant have done this if he was already two and a half years into pretrial and he hadn't agreed to testify against Shawn yet? In addition, Shawn points out the example the District Court uses for impaired defense - the loss of exculpatory witnesses - is exactly what happened during this crucial eight month period. The witness Erick Castillo (and his brother) left the country. The District Court's holding that "Gardner's testimony and Castillo's testimony Note also that petitioner's co-defendant's decision to accept a deal and testify against petitioner was made after it was determined that the only two other witnesses against petitioner and the codefendant had fled to Mexico and were not available for trial. This makes the State's speculation that Gardner would have suddenly decided to testify against petitions at that point all the more unlikely. The District Court's citation to United States v. Lam, 251F.3d852,860(9thCir.2001) are also off point. In petitioner's case there is no speculation about lost evidence or defects in witness testimony were consistent with regard to petitioner" is factually wrong. (Opinion 20:17-18) Gardner's testimony that he and Shawn followed the two young men who actually entered the home and killed the victim by only fifteen feet would possibly be consistent with all four of them traveling essentially together. Castillo's testimony that Shawn and Gardner were following by about fifty yards makes it nearly impossible to assert that the four were traveling together or communicating. Since the only reason petition is in prison is because of the inference that he and Gardner aided and abetted in the killing necessitates that there was some agreement to act together (even if simply by acting as "lookouts"), their proximity to the two who actually killed the victim is a huge matter. It shows Shawn and Gardner were too far behind the others to communicate an intention at the moment and Gardner had already testified there was no agreement, explicit or tacit, prior to the crime. Gardner actually testified that Shawn entered the victim's home and that Shawn went through the victim's kitchen drawers. Gardner testified he then left the window at the side of the victim's home and went back to stand in front of the house where Shawn joined him. Castillo testified that Shawn and Gardner left the side yard together. This is significant because the question of whether Shawn aided and abetted in the robbery and/or burglary is not proven even by Gardner's testimony and so the State needs to imply some overt act by Shawn which indicates an agreement, encouragement or help offered by Shawn to Rivera and Pena in order to support Shawn's conviction. If he did not enter the home and take something then it's impossible to imply Shawn showed any behavior which indicated aiding and abetting in Rivera and Pena's robbery and burglary. Because of this a significant part of the State's case against Shawn was the assertion that Shawn stole chocolate liquors from the victim's kitchen. Gardner claims he saw Shawn enter the kitchen and watched Shawn while he was in there, but Gardner didn't see Shawn take anything. Gardner claims when he saw Shawn again that Shawn had nothing in his hands nor did he appear to have anything in his pockets. The State's only claim is that Shawn stole the chocolates during the period after Gardner watched him entire the kitchen and after he Gardner walked away. But if Castillo is telling the truth, Gardner and Shawn left together, which means there was no time at which Shawn was in the victim's kitchen without Gardner watching him. Which means according to Gardner's testimony, Gardner didn't see Shawn take anything from the victim from the moment Shawn entered the home to the moment Shawn left the home. This is significant. That only way the State can explain this is to insist Gardner left prior to Shawn leaving the home so there was a period when Shawn wasn't being observed.(Opinion,20:14-21:17). The District Court's analysis of Shawn's right to a speedy trial is flawed by the District Court's determination that Shawn's consent to prior extensions somehow creates a waiver to any and all claims of delay. This flaw is facilitated by the Court's decision to consider the entire 42 months between the time Shawn was arrested and the time he went to trial instead of the eight months during which Shawn asked five times for severance due to delays, and during which time Shawn claims prejudice. The District Court's analysis is also flawed by the Court's correct holding that prejudice cannot be speculative, and then the Court's assertion as to what Shawn's co-defendant might or might not have done had Shawn not suffered delay. The Court's analysis is also flawed by unintelligible speculation that Shawn's co-defendant might have spontaneously decided to testify against Shawn after the only witnesses fled to Mexico, before the police discovered incriminating tapes against the co-defendant, and after two and a half years of pretrial during which there is no evidence the co-defendant ever considered a deal. Certainly a reasonable jurist could debate or disagree with the

District Court's analysis and Shawn has made a substantial showing of the denial of a Constitutional right and certainly this issue is adequate to deserve encouragement to proceed further Issue Two: Was petitioner's right to effective assistance of counsel violated when his attorney failed to ask that the jury be instructed in the availability of a lesser inclusive offense of Second Degree murder because he claimed this was a trial tactic while never asking for nor realizing that Second Degree felony murder was lesser inclusive offenses about which the jury should have been instructed?

The District Court analyzes the question of Shawn's counsel's effectiveness based upon his decision to not have the jury instructed about the lesser inclusive offense of second degree murder. But this is not what happened. The District Court's opinion shows the two attorneys and the judge were talking on the record not only about second degree murder but also second degree felony murder. (Opinion, 22:17-23:21) The discourse clearly shows that is what the prosecutor is describing (at 21:21-23) when the defense counsel asks for clarification of the differences between first degree and second degree. The prosecutor answers, "Well, the first is just based on straight felony murder. The second is based on aiding and abetting a murder that someone is doing based on wanton disregard for human life." The Court goes on to further clarify that the Court, too, understands that there are not just talking about second degree murder, but also about second degree felony murder. "Okay. So [petitioner] would either have to have the intent to kill himself, "which would have been second degree murder, "or he would have to have ... [an] ample state of implied malice meaning that he intentionally committed an act, the natural consequence of the act was dangerous to human life, and he knew the act was dangerous to human life and acted with conscious disregard in encouraging, facilitating, aiding or abetting [the two young men who actually killed the victim]," which is the definition of second degree felony murder. (Opinion,21:18-28) Shawn's counsel ultimately decided not to ask for a jury instruction on second degree murder because he determined that he would actually have to start arguing that petitioner had the intent to kill. This decision appears to be a trial tactic. Unfortunately petitioner's counsel does not realize that he can still ask for the jury instruction on second degree felony murder, which does not require an intent to kill.

The District Court determined there is no Federal jurisdiction to look at the question as to whether the Court itself should have given the instruction. (25:10-26) It then looks at the ineffective assistance of counsel argument. "[U]nder Strickland [v. Washington, 466 U.S. 668, (1984)] petitioner first must prove that his attorney's representation fell below an objective standard of reasonableness by identifying the acts or omissions

that rendered the representation objectively
unreasonable. Id. at 687-88, 690."(Opinion26:4-6)
But the District Court then analyzes Shawn's
counsel's decision to not ask for the second degree
murder instruction, not the failure to realize he
could have asked for the second degree felony
murder instruction. Although the court determines
Shawn's counsel's decision not to ask for the
second degree murder instruction was a reasonable
trial tactic, certainly the failure of Shawn's counsel
to even realize the difference between second
degree murder and second degree felony murder is
not. Not only does Shawn's counsel not understand
that second degree murder and second degree
felony murder are different, he's actually asking
the prosecutor to explain it to him. In addition,
although Shawn's trial counsel is correct that in
order for the jury to determine Shawn was
innocent of first degree felony murder but guilty of
second degree murder, they would have to
conclude that Shawn did not have the intent to rob

or burgle but he did have the intent to kill the victim. Shawn's counsel says "…I don't plan to get up there and say that [petitioner] in any way agreed to engage in a homicide of Mr. Love and it sounds like that's almost what I have to argue." But there is no indication that Shawn's counsel would have actively had to argue that Shawn intended to kill the victim. The jury instruction would have merely given the jury the ability to determine themselves, against the arguments of Shawn's counsel, that Shawn had intended not to rob or burgle but did intent to kill. Shawn's counsel should have realized there was nothing in the jury instruction that demanded that he try to convince the jury his client intended to kill, just as the jury instructions about felony murder didn't demand that Shawn's counsel try to convince the jury Shawn intended to rob or burgle. It was not a reasonable trial tactic for Shawn's counsel to not realize he did not have to actively argue Shawn intended to kill the victim, but that this would allow the jury to make that determination against counsel's arguments but perhaps to Shawn's advantage. Whether Shawn's counsel didn't realize the difference between second degree murder and second degree felony murder, or whether he didn't realize a jury instruction regarding second degree murder did not mean he'd have to argue his client intended to kill, certainly the first prong of the Strickland test is satisfied. The second prong is that Shawn must show he was actually prejudiced by the deficiency. In this case we have the jury itself sending a note to the judge asking if there were any lesser inclusive crimes for which they could sentence Shawn. (25:27) this is proof that the jury was having trouble with the first degree felony murder conviction and was looking for something less. Certainly this indicates that Shawn was prejudiced by the lack of such a lesser inclusive offence for the jury to look at. Because the District Court did not look at Shawn's counsel's decision to not ask for a jury instruction on second degree felony murder, the District Court did not analyze that deficiency. A reasonable jurist could disagree with the District Court's analysis. Shawn Khalifa deserves encouragement to proceed further. Issue Three: Was it ineffective assistance of counsel for petitioner's attorney to allow the trial court to instruct his jury that petitioner's co-defendant was an accomplice as a 'matter of law?' The District Court points out, correctly, that there is a more stringent jury instruction regarding adverse accomplice testimony. (29:7-30:12)The District Court then asserts that because of this, the trial court's instruction to Shawn's jury that the testifying co-defendant was an accomplished was harmless because if the jury had determined Shawn's co-defendant was not an accomplice they would have been allowed to treat his testimony without balancing his possible personal motives for testifying against Shawn, which would have arguably given the co-dependent's testimony even more weight. The District Court determined that failure to object to the jury instruction regarding Gardner being an accomplice 'as a matter of law' did not constitute ineffective assistance of counsel because Shawn can not show that this action prejudiced him. (34:24-35:2) Shawn had argued that the jury was told Gardner was an accomplice 'as a matter of law' simply for watching his friends walk in the front door of a house, waiting outside for them to come out, and after a while going around to the side of the house to look in through a window to see what was happening. The jury was also informed that this behavior (highly questionable as even amounting to aiding abetting) was enough to make Gardner 'an accomplice as a matter of law.' This means the jury was tacitly being instructed that Shawn was also an accomplice 'as a matter of law' for merely watching two young men walk in the front door of a house, waiting for them to come out, and then walking around to the side of the house to look in a window to see what was happening. The District

Court determined that this wasn't prejudicial in the Federal Habeas context. ("[P]etitioner is not entitled to [Federal] habeas relief unless an error in the instructions had a "substantial and injurious effect or influence in determining the jury's verdict."" (30:3-7)) The District Court determined Shawn has not met this high burden. This is because the Court determined Shawn's participation was (by Gardner's account) greater than Gardner. (33:15-19) But this is the whole reason that telling the jury that Gardner is an accomplice in murder 'as a matter of law' is so prejudicial. It amounted to a directed verdict. What's more, the District Court then recites a whole litany of circumstantial evidence which the Court claims could have corroborated Gardner's testimony (but none of which corroborates Gardner's claims that Shawn entered the victim's home). But this simply proves this decision wasn't a reasonable trial tactic. Leaving the determination in the hands of the jury would have had no down side - whether they determined Gardner wasn't an accomplice (in which case his testimony would have been given the same weight as any other witness) or whether they determined he was an accomplice (in which case his testimony would be corroborated and then given the same weight as any other witness). Therefore, claiming this was a reasonable trial tactic doesn't pass examination. What's more, all the 'evidence' the District Court points to is all circumstantial evidence, none of which proves Shawn had either an agreement with the two young men who killed the victim, or that Shawn aided or abetted in any manner, or that he entered the victim's home. Which leaves all the arguments Shawn originally put forth - that his trial court told the jury that Gardner was an accomplice 'as a matter of law' despite the fact Gardner was going to testify that Shawn's participation was at least the same as Gardner's own, and then the trial court was going to ask the jury to determine whether Shawn was an accomplice. This is horrifically prejudicial. And this is why no reasonable attorney would have chosen this as a trial tactic: even if the jury was told Gardner was a co-defendant and they didn't believe a single thing he said, the other evidence indicates Shawn did no more than Gardner did... which the trial court told the jury made Gardner an accomplice 'as a matter of law.' For an error in giving or failing to give a jury instruction to rise to a federal constitutional dimension it must amount to a structural defect. When that happens it is reversible per se. (Sullivan v. Louisiana (1993) 508 U.S. 275; see Harmon v. Marshall (9th Cir. 1995) 69 F.3d 963) an error in an instruction that amounts to a directed verdict is exactly the kind of structural defect requiring reversal per se. Although not expressly listed as a structural defect, the United States Supreme Court has indicated in dicta that this type of error is probably reversible per se because it would altogether deny the Sixth Amendment right to trial by jury. (See Rose v.

Clark (1986) 478 U.S. 570, 578; see also United States v. Martin Linen Supply Co. (1977) 430 U.S. 564, 572-573; People v. Jarrell (1987)196Cal.App.3d604, 607-608.) And, the Ninth Circuit has since held that instructing in a way that amounts to a directed verdict is, in fact, a structural defect requiring reversal per se on federal habeas corpus. (Powell v. Galaza (9th Cir. 2003) 328 F.3d 558 (structural defect to instruct jury that defendant's own testimony satisfied specific intent element of crime). Certainly a reasonable jurist could disagree with the District Court's analysis. Shawn Khalifa has made a substantial showing of the possibility of the denial of a Constitutional right and certainly this issue is adequate to deserve encouragement to proceed further.

Issue Four: Is there insufficient evidence to support Shawn's conviction for first degree felony murder? Ineffective assistance of counsel. Was it ineffective assistance of counsel for petitioner's lawyer not to insist on separate verdict forms in order to ensure unanimity as to the specific predicate offense for the felony murder? (Shawn has advanced a claim of ineffective assistance of counsel throughout the State Court appeal process as well as in his Federal Habeas Petition to the Federal District Court)

The US Supreme Court has held that allowing jurors to adopt different theories of an offense in order to come to a unanimous consensus as to the end crime is not a violation of a person's right to be found guilty only by a unanimous jury. (Schad v. Arizona, 501U.S.624 (1991),Mullaneyv. Wilbur, 421U.S.684, 690-691(1975)) Just the same, the Supreme Court pointed out this is only because legislatures often define different ways of committing the same offense. The question is whether we are talking about two different means of committing the same offense, or whether we are talking about two means that are "so disparate as to exemplify two inherently separate offenses."

(Schad, at 643) The question becomes, are the two mental states supposed to be equivalent means to satisfy the element of a single offense? In Shawn's case we are literally talking about two separate offenses which are not interchangeable: robbery and burglary. What's more, these two underlying offenses are materially opposite in many significant ways. Burglary demands a specific state of mind (breaking into a home with intent to commit a felony) and it is irrelevant whether the intended felony is committed once the breaking-in has occurred. Robbery, in contrast, necessitates no prior intent, but it demands that a taking actually transpire. In Shawn's case, allowing individual Shawn's jurors to find different underlying offense is not merely to allow them to find different means to an end but to allow them to disagree on whether there was any intent to commit a felony at all, and to disagree as to whether there was any felony committed once inside the home. When the evidence in the case, if believed by the jury, shows that the defendant committed several acts, any of which could support a finding of guilty of the particular act charged, the defense is generally entitled, on demand at the start of trial, to have the prosecution elect on which of several distinct acts it is relying for each individual charge. (People v. Salvato (1991)234Cal.App.3d872, 878-879) If the prosecution does not elect any specific act on which to rely to prove the charge and does not prove any specific offense, the court must instruct the jury that it must unanimously agree that the defendant committed the same act or acts. (People v. Davis (2005) 36 Cal. 4th 510; People v. Norman (2007) 157 Cal. App. 4th 460, (unanimity instruction required when evidence shows two separate acts and prosecutor has not made election); People v. Melendez (1990) 224 Cal. App. 3d 1420, 1428-1434; People v. Wesley (1986) 177 Cal. App. 3d 397, 401-402; see also People v. King (1991) 231Cal.App.3d493, 501-502.) This applies especially if the defendant is charged with one count based on either of two acts, and the defendant has a separate defense for each act. (People v. Davis (2005) 36 Cal. 4th 510; People v. Castaneda (1997) 55 Cal. App. 4th 1067.) This requirement typically applies to acts that could have been charged as separate offenses. For example, the case where a single charged burglary may be based on either the entry into the home or the entry into a bedroom after having entered the home, depending on when the defendant's intent to commit theft or a felony arose, the evidence concerns the theory of liability for the single burglary and no unanimity instruction is needed as to which entry is found by the jurors. (People v. Taylor (2010)48Cal.4th574) The US Supreme Court jokes in their Schad v. Arizona opinion that "nothing in our history suggests that the Due Process Clause would permit a State to convict anyone under a charge of "Crime" so generic that any combination of jury findings of embezzlement, reckless driving, murder, burglary, tax evasion, or littering, for example, would suffice for conviction." (Supra at 633) But this is the case we are looking at - due to the nature of the felony murder rule, once Rivera and Pena killed the victim, Shawn's guilt in that first degree murder was to be determined entirely upon the presence or absence of completely different underlying felonies. If this logic stands, then the more felonies the State charged Shawn with, the easier it will be to convict him because they don't need more than a handful of jurors to believe him guilty of any of the underlying felonies. Certainly Shawn Khalifa has made a substantial showing of the denial of a Constitutional right and certainly this issue is adequate to deserve encouragement to proceed further.

Issue Five: In light of the US Supreme Court's decision in Miller v. Arizona, was petitioner's conviction for felony murder and subsequent sentence of 25 years to life after being direct-filed to adult court by the prosecutor in a process that never took into consideration an individualized assessment of petitioner's age or the extent of his involvement in the offense, constitute cruel and unusual punishment?

The District Court claims Shawn's issue was "that his sentence is cruel and unusual because of "his level of participation in the offense, his age [at the time of the offense], his prior offense of attempting to steal beer, and his demonstrated ability to reform."(Pet.Mem.at23)."(Opinion, 47:20-22) The District Court determined that the State court's holding that Shawn's sentence was not unconstitutional, "was not contrary to, or an unreasonable application of, the Supreme Court's cruel and unusual punishment jurisprudence."(Opinion, 46:2-4) The District Court points out that Shawn in not in a position to claim any of the categorical exclusions under the Eighth Amendment as established by United States Supreme Court precedent. (46:5-6) The District

Court then claims (1), "The Court is not aware of any authority from the Supreme Court establishing that it is cruel and unusual punishment under the Eighth Amendment to impose a sentence of 25yearstolifefor first degree murder committed while the defendant was 15 years old,"3 (46:14-16)and(2), "Even if the Supreme Court's reasoning in Graham [v. Florida, 130 S. Ct. 2011(2010)]concerning their deduced moral culpability of juvenile offenders as compared with adults supports petitioner's argument, Graham was decided in 2010, three years after petitioner's conviction, and the Court is not aware of any authority from the Supreme Court or the Ninth Circuit that has made Graham applicable retroactively to cases on collateral review. Thus, Graham is not applicable to petitioner's claim on federal habeas review. See Williams, 529 U.S. at 380 (federal habeas courts "must deny relief that is contingent upon a rule of law not clearly established at the time the state conviction became final").""(Opinion,pg46,FN5) as shown above, petitioner's actual claim was that it was cruel and unusual because of his level of participation in the offense, his age (15 years old), his prior act of stealing beer, and his demonstrated ability to reform.(Opinion,47:20-22) Thus the District Court's holding is based upon two beliefs; (1) Shawn's claim depends on the presence of a US Supreme Court holdings regarding the imposition of a 25-to-life sentence for first degree murder for a defendant who was 15 years old, and (2) the US Supreme Court case law indicating a reduced moral culpability for juvenile offenders as compared with adults is based entirely on Graham and there is no other US Supreme Court precedence for this prior to 2010 and it is therefore "new law" not established at the time of Shawn's offense. Both of these beliefs have now been proven false by the US Supreme Court's opinion in Millerv .Alabama (No.10–9646),decided three days ago(June25,2012). As for the first of the

District Court's assertions, that past US Supreme Court case haven't determined anything in regard to 25-to-life sentences for 15-year olds - this is an erroneously narrow reading of the US Supreme Court decisions. As the Supreme Court states in Miller, the Arkansas Supreme Court also determined "that Roper [v. Simmons, 543 U. S. 551, (2005)] and Graham were "narrowly tailored" to their contexts: "death-penalty cases involving a juvenile and life-imprisonment-without-parole cases for non-homicide offenses involving a juvenile."" But the Court in Miller drew a much broader interpretation of their past holdings regarding juveniles. The Miller opinion held that the prohibition of cruel and unusual punishment "guarantees individuals the right not to be subjected to excessive sanctions," (Roper v. Simmons, 543 U. S. 551, 560) and that this right "flows from the basic precept of justice that punishment for crime should be graduated and proportioned" to both the offender and the offense.

(id.) The Court held that its opinions in Roper and Graham (supra) establish that juveniles are constitutionally different from adults for sentencing purposes. Their "lack of maturity" and "underdeveloped sense of responsibility" lead to recklessness, impulsivity, and heedless risk-taking. (Roper, at 569). They "are more vulnerable . . . to negative influences and outside pressures," including from their family and peers. They have limited "contro[l] over their own environment" and lack the ability to extricate themselves from horrific, crime-producing settings and because a child's character is not as "well formed" as an adult's, his traits are "less fixed" and his actions are less likely to be "evidence of irretrievable depravity" Id., at 570. The Court held that its decisions in Roper and Graham emphasized that the distinctive attributes of youth diminish the penological justifications for imposing the harshest sentences on juvenile offenders, even when they commit terrible crimes. What's more, the Court goes on to say that although their decision in Graham concerned life-without-parole cases, nothing that Graham said about children - their distinctive (and transitory) mental traits and environmental vulnerabilities - is crime specific. In fact, the Court goes on to say explicitly that ""An offender's age," we made clear in Graham, "is relevant to the Eighth Amendment," and so "criminal procedure laws that fail to take defendants' youthfulness into account at all would be flawed."" The reason the Court banned automatic life-without-parole schemes for juveniles was because "By removing youth from the balance... these laws prohibit a sentencing authority from assessing whether the law's harshest term of imprisonment proportionately punishes a juvenile offender. That contravenes Graham's (and also Roper's) foundational principle: that imposition of a State's most severe penalties on juvenile offenders cannot proceed as though they were not children." And this is the whole point. The California criminal process which tried and sentenced Shawn Khalifa was automatic and denied him any chance at having his age taken into account or having an individualized assessment. The Court held that mandatory penalty schemes prevent the trial court from considering youth and from assessing whether the law's harshest term of imprisonment proportionately punishes a juvenile offender. The Court holds that this contradicts Graham's (and also Roper's) foundational principle: that imposition of a State's most severe penalties on juvenile offenders cannot proceed as though they were not children.

In addition, the District Court's reliance upon Harmelin v. Michigan, 501 U. S. 957, is completely dismantled by the Court in Miller. Harmelin has nothing to do with juveniles and the Court has held on multiple occasions that sentencing practices that are permissible for adults may not be so for juveniles. (Roper, supra; Graham, supra) As for the second of the District

Court's assertions, that any implications to be drawn from the US Supreme Court's opinion in Graham regarding the moral culpability of juveniles is "new law" established in Graham and therefore not available to Shawn whose offense happened prior to the Graham determination - the Court in Miller asserts the opposite. The Miller opinion starts by pointing out that the interest in proportionality in sentencing and how that affects juvenile sentencing, did not originate in Graham but is the product of long established principles. The Court holds that these mandatory penalty schemes "contravenes Graham's (and also Roper's) foundational principle: that imposition of a State's most severe penalties on juvenile offenders cannot proceed as though they were not children." The Court then goes on to show that this foundational principle is not "new law," but is well established. "Of special pertinence here, we insisted in these rulings that a sentencer have the ability to consider the "mitigating qualities of youth." Johnson v. Texas, 509 U. S. 350, 367 (1993). Everything we said in Roper and Graham about that stage of life also appears in these decisions. As we observed, "youth is more than a chronological fact." Eddings [v. Oklahoma, 455 U. S. 104, (1982)] at 115. It is a time of immaturity, irresponsibility, "impetuousness [,] and recklessness." Johnson, 509 U. S., at 368. It is a moment and "condition of life when a person may be most susceptible to influence and to psychological damage." Eddings, 455 U. S., at 115. And its "signature qualities" are all "transient." Johnson, 509 U. S., at 368. Eddings is especially on point. There, a 16-year-old shot a police officer point-blank and killed him. We invalidated his death sentence because the judge did not consider evidence of his neglectful and violent family background (including his mother's drug abuse and his father's physical abuse) and his emotional disturbance. We found that evidence "particularly relevant"—more so than it would have been in the case of an adult offender. 455 U. S., at 115. We held: "[J]ust as the chronological age of a minor is itself a relevant mitigating factor of great weight, so must the background and mental and emotional development of a youthful defendant be duly considered" in assessing his culpability. Id., at 116."These cases all show that the case law concerning the 'moral culpability' of minors in US Supreme Court precedence precede not just Roper and Graham, but they clearly precede Shawn Khalifa's trial and offence. Is a sentence of 25 years to life cruel and unusual punishment for the actions ofa15-year-old if sentenced without individualized assessment of petitioner? Although the District Court frames the question as whether there is any US Supreme Court holdings regarding the imposition of a25-to-life sentence for murder for a 15-year-old, the real question is whether the US Supreme Court has any holdings which support the necessity of a process which takes into account of a juvenile's particular circumstances instead of treating them automatically as adults. The Court explicitly points out that under these systems, "every juvenile will receive the same sentence as every other — the 17-year-old and the 14-year-old, the shooter and the accomplice..." (Emphasis added) Not only was Shawn Khalifa denied individualized assessment as a juvenile, but he was sentenced under the felony-murder law in which the fact that the jury apparently determined he had implicitly agreed to act as a 'lookout' made him guilty of first degree murder. The Court then goes on to criticize the use of prosecutorial schemes that leave the decision to try a juvenile as an adult up to the prosecutor. This was the process by which both the defendants in Miller ended up in adult court, and this is exactly the manner in whichShawnKhalifawastriedinadultcourtattheageof 15. Also, just as with the two defendants in Miller, Shawn Khalifa was faced with a system where the "sentencing authority [did not] have any discretion to impose a different punishment. State law mandated [the sentence] even if a judge or jury would have thought that his youth and its attendant characteristics, along with the nature of his crime, made a lesser sentence… more appropriate. Such a scheme prevents those meting out punishment from considering a juvenile's "lessened culpability" and greater "capacity for change…"" Just as the defendant in Miller (Jackson) faced a system where he was ineligible for the death penalty due to his age and therefore the life-without-parole sentence was "mandatory," so was Shawn Khalifa faced with the identical situation where both the death penalty and life-without-parole were statutorilybarredandthereforethe"mandatory"penaltywas25-to-life.

Is prosecution for felony murder against a 15-year-old juvenile cruel and unusual punishment if done without individualized assessment of petitioner? The Court goes on to undermine any implication that the justifications for the felony-murder doctrine are applicable to juveniles. "Nor can deterrence do the work in this context, because "'the same characteristics that render juveniles less culpable than adults'"—their immaturity, recklessness, and impetuosity—make them less likely to consider potential punishment.(Graham,quotingRoper,supraat571) The Court goes on to say their determination in Miller is based upon a realization that such sentencing schemes neglect "the circumstances of the homicide offense, including the extent of his participation in the conduct and the way familial and peer pressures may have affected him…" And this is the problem with the felony-murder rule in general. It is doubly oppressive when put upon a 15-year-old who by all accounts was guilty of nothing more than the curiosity of youth and the immaturity to realize how to handle a situation which developed in a way he had not agreed to participate in. As the Court says in Miller,

"Grahamand Roperandour individualized sentencing cases alike teach that in imposing a State's harshest penalties, a sentencer misses too much if he treats every child as an adult."

Certainly Shawn Khalifa has made a substantial showing of the denial of a Constitutional right and certainly these issues deserve encouragement to proceed further.

Conclusion Petitioner's issues, particularly those in light of the US Supreme Court's Miller decision, certainly deserve his being given the opportunity to brief the Circuit Court on them and to further develop the issues and the arguments.

_____ _____ Date

JAMESW.WHITEHOUSE Attorney for Petitioner SHAWNMALONEKHALIFA

CHAPTER 4

These issues were denied at appeal and we had to submit a certificate of Appeal ability to the 9th circuit court. The issue accepted was the right to a speedy trial.

We were granted the certificate of appeal-ability for the right to a speedy trial, but lost the appeal one judge agreed but the other two did not. In our documents were facts that supported the DA carelessly and recklessly losing contact with the Castillo Brothers, as witnesses the judge in the transcripts states disappointment in their lack of any attempt to produce the brothers as witnesses for several concrete reasons: One of the brothers at pre-trial told the same story that Shawn did and would make a better witness for the defense. He would impeach Marks statements and be a strong avenue for Shawn's getting a fair trial. The DA were proven to lack motivation to force the two to testify at trial throughout the documents.

I wish so much in my heart that there is a good ending to this story but sadly there isn't, we have exhausted our appeals up the Supreme Court. There is relief for persons who actually commit murder and were given life without parole sentences. For kids like Shawn with 25 years to life there is no relief. It is a reality that Fernando Rivera the known murderer could be out of prison before Shawn. At this point in time a person who was found guilty of murder was released after spending 14 years of his term. Shawn has presently served 12 years. Mark the kid that was by Shawn's side the entire time of the crime is now out of prison and about. It is a sad reality that lying and trickery pay's off while strength of character is punished severely. One should ask themselves why SB 260, SB 261 does not relieve the young victims of the felony murder rule.

Youth that did not commit murder and are were under the age of 16 at the time of the crime, are the kids that received the harshest penalties. I continue to maintain the opinion that prison is a big business a captive youth for 25 years provides the state that many years' worth of money and support for our children; a family will go without to provide money that insures relief for their child, no matter the exorbitant mark ups and this money will be supplied at any cost to the family. When a child is imprisoned the family is also in prison.

EPILOG

Shawn has proven to be a brilliant author and poet, he mentors others: prisoners and youth at risk, see pensideout.org his organization which provides the guidance that aids youths at risk through knowledge and advice that will keep them from experiencing his dire straits. His objective is to educate and cut the potential for crime off at the pass. He is a strong, caring and loving person who I know will change the world if given a chance.

Become Mother Love is a message I was given. I have fulfilled this plan for me by providing the world with my two great children, Jenny as a health educator and Shawn as an author; this

experience is theirs to tell; and the objective is to

make changes to the world in God's name and on

his terms.

The outstanding messages I have gotten

are:

- Oprah, which I had years ago and actually wrote her, I felt it was silly but no rock should be left unturned. Recently a huge supporter Marissa Presley, an angel in her own right was watching an interview given by Oprah to Mr. Brian Stevenson (Equal justice Initiative) an advocate for protecting youth that are the victims of our society. Thank you, Marissa for all you are doing and have done for the Khalifa and Ponce families. Hopefully Mr. Brian Stevenson will be convinced to join our team.

- I have heard the words, National Clemency for many years.

- The last message is January.

As far as the messages go reference back to book one, I have just heard a sermon on Catholic TV mass and it was: You enter into oneness with Jesus through baptism in water. "Never one on earth but in eternity and one on earth but not in heaven", through the sacrifice on the cross and the sacraments we become one with Jesus. At the last supper Jesus said Remember me. This is how I interpret the messages from my Brother Bob. Everyone has to live by their own personal belief. I have concluded that we continue to learn and grow in heaven, when we leave we are the same person that we were on earth. For some reason I believe there are multiple spirits for one being. Is this what makes us Christ like???????

I am but a humble servant and with the Grace of God, will be blessed with the return of my son, so that he can accomplish his destiny on earth in Jesus's name. Please pray with us. Thank You Jesus for letting me be a part of Shawn Khalifa completing Gods plan for him.

We continue to hold onto our hopes and dreams please head this compassionate plea and help us right a wrong and free Shawn Khalifa.

This is a letter that he has written to the Students that I would like to share with you.
TO THE STUDENTS

I am an inmate serving a life sentence in a California state prison. I was incarcerated (locked up) when I was 15 years old. My 16-year old friend went to rob a house and he ended up beating the owner to death. That same friend shot and killed an 18-year old kid who helped him rob that house. I was convicted of murder for the man who died in the house robbery. I am now 27 years old and going to die in prison. I'm writing this letter because I know how it feels to kick it with the homies and have respect from them. I'm telling you the truth when I write that's not the respect we need. I was raised by a single mother.

She is who I should have been living for, not my homies.

If you're not paying attention to this, you're the kid I'm trying to reach. People tried to reach me but I did not let them. Let this letter reach you, because you're the reason I'm writing this. I remember I hated my school teachers but I later learned in juvenile hall that they are some of the most important people in our cities. Have you have ever taken the time to think about the reasons your teacher is a teacher in the first place? Because of you. To teach you what you're not going to learn from the homies. Knowledge is more power than a gang will ever have. When you get home today try to find some time to talk to your parents, grandparents or whoever is raising you. Tell them how much you love them and give them a big hug. That person will be the first, and last person to stand by you. They're there when your born, they'll be their when you die. My mother has visited me almost every week for the past 7-years. Even when I was sent over 1,000 miles away from home to Pelican Bay State Prison she found her way there to visit me. Now even though I'm going to die in prison I want to earn my mother's respect, not the homies. The homies led me to a life prison sentence. You are important to the world. Being from the gettho only makes you stronger for doing something with your life. Education is key. If you find yourself in prison in the future you can think back to this letter, and remember I tried to tell you. If you find yourself outside with the homies look to the sky to remind yourself there is more to life! Don't do it. You are the only one who can stop yourself from doing well. You are. Your worst enemy is yourself not the kid from a different gang. If you want a better life make one for yourself. It's really up to you.

Shawn has written several books for misguided teens; you can find them on Amazon they are:

Proposition 21

My Bleeding Pen

You Won't Like It Here

Bear Flag Prisoner